'SCALE

A True Account of a Signalman in the British Army

To,

John,

From one Scaley
to another.

All the best

Pete Molloy

30·10·22

FINIAL PUBLISHING

First published 2008
FINIAL PUBLISHING

ISBN 978-1-900467-38-4

Produced by Finial Publishing
15 Abingdon Drive
Caversham Park
Reading
RG4 6SA
Telephone: 01189 484103
Email: mail@finial.co.uk
www.finial.co.uk

Acknowledgements

I would like to thank three people who have helped me with this book, first, Barry, another Ex Squaddie, for his more in depth knowledge of the English language than me. Last but not least, another Ex Squaddie Tony for his patience and the use of his computer.

I would really like to thank my American cousin, Anthony Aliberti, author of *Shark, The Baker's Son,* for if it was not for his knowledge and skill in writing and his encouragement, then this book would still be far from completion.

Dedication

This book is dedicated to my two children, Natasha and Ryan.

Scaley

(Operation Granby)

'Scaley' came from the word 'Scaleyback,' which is a word that was often used by the members of other Regiments and Corps of the British army as a nickname for members of the Royal Corps of Signals. Nevertheless, the likelihood was that no one really knew its exact true origins.

There were many stories in existence: One popular idea concerned behind 'Scaley' was that they were early backpack radios, although a second notion was the radios were powered by lead-acid batteries and had been prone to leakage, consequently, scarring the backs of the radio operators, another suggestion was early linemen may have worn body armour, of some description, on their backs as a form of protection when they were bending forward to lay or repair radio lines, a further alternative was the headquarters of one of the earlier Signals units was housed above a fish market, and an extension to this headquarters was that in Normandy, during World War II in 1944, a Signals unit was billeted in a fish-canning factory, and, as a result, the soldiers had to sleep on the floor of the factory amongst the many layers of discarded fish scales, and, finally, the suggestion on the highest authority, a Sergeant Major in the Corps during the early 1920's, was most plausible; 'Scaleyback' was a colloquial term for a disease in horses caused by ill-fitting saddles or harness equipment in which our context was aimed at people who did not look after or used their horses properly. Indeed, the Corps last used horse-drawn cable layers in the year 1937.

The Gulf War
Key events in the crisis

2 August 1990: At 02.00 hours, Iraqi tanks and troops invade Kuwait, taking Kuwait City. UN Resolution 660 condemns Iraq's invasion of Kuwait.

6 August: UN Resolution 661 effectively imposes trade embargo on Iraq.

10 August: UN Resolution 662 unanimously condemns Iraq's annexation of Kuwait.

28 August: Iraqi Presidential Decree declares Kuwait Iraq's Nineteenth Province.

1 September: Freed Western women and children start to leave Iraq.

9 September: Helsinki summit between US President George Bush and Soviet President Mikhail Gorbachev: leaders agree on plan to deal with Iraq.

29 November: UN Resolution 678 authorizes member states to 'use all necessary means' to make Iraq comply with previous resolutions.

6 December: Saddam Hussein announces release of Western hostages.

9 January 1991: talks between US Secretary of State George Baker and Iraqi Foreign Minister Tarek Aziz in Geneva fail to make any progress.

12 January: UN Secretary General, Javier Perez de Cuellar, makes final attempt to negotiate with Saddam Hussein. Talks fail.

15 January: UN deadline for Iraqi withdrawal from Kuwait. Iraqi forces do not retreat.

17 January: 02.00hours, Allied air bombardment of Iraq begins.

30 January: Iraqi forces capture Khafji and hold it for just over a day, before retreating.

15 February: Iraq's Revolutionary Command Council announces that Iraqi forces would leave Kuwait in accordance with UN Resolutions ... but only on certain conditions, which are unacceptable to the Allies.

22 February: US agrees that if an unambiguous Iraqi withdrawal begins by 20.00 hours, hostilities could end. No Iraqi withdrawal.

24 February: 04.00 hours. Land attack begins.

27 February: Kuwait City liberated. Iraq's forces in Kuwait largely destroyed, dispersed or captured.

28 February: 08.00 hours. President Bush orders a cease-fire and hostilities end.

3 March: All the Allied terms for making cease-fire permanent are accepted by Iraqis.

3 April: UN Resolution 687 formally ends Gulf war. Iraq accepts condition.

Reproduced from: The Gulf War (Revised Edition) by Dr. John King.
1991 Wayland (Publishers) Limited.

Peter Molloy, photographed at 8 Sigs for
Satisfied Soldier in Liverpool Army Careers Office, 1990.

1

I was born in Liverpool on the 9th of November 1970 and spent the first few years of my life living in either my granddad's bottom floor council flat in Childwall on my dad's side or my Nan and granddad's upstairs council maisonette in Aigburth on my mam's side. We finally moved into a bottom floor council maisonette on the Belle Vale estate in the southern area of Liverpool when I was about three years old. These were the days before the 'right to buy' your council home made it possible for many working class people to become home owners. So, many people, when they got married, lived with their parents until they were offered council accommodation by the city council. Meanwhile, in August of 1977, I was six years old and just returned from my first ever holiday, visiting my Auntie Mary, who was my dad's sister, along with the rest of our family living in Pittsburgh, Pennsylvania in the United States of America. Upon our return home, the council gave us a bungalow on our estate due to my dad's disability. My dad could not walk properly and had trouble climbing stairs.

The year was 1980, and I was nine years old when my mam informed my dad and me that she was leaving us. I remember being devastated and crying my eyes out at the thought of my mam not living with us anymore. She turned to me and asked me whom I wanted to live with, and I chose to live with my dad instead because my dad treated me much better than my mam ever did. In fact, it materialised a few months later that my mam had been having an affair with one of my dad's friend's brother. She married the man to whom she was having the affair with and had a son to him. On the other hand, my father remarried in 1982. His new wife did not have any children of her own, and they remained living in the same bungalow on Belle Vale estate. I stayed there until my late teens before re-enlisting into the army.

Reflecting back to when I was five years old and in the first year infants at Craighurst County Primary School in Liverpool, I was sitting in a classroom with all of my classmates receiving a talk from a policeman about not talking to strangers. From that point on, I decided that I wanted to become a policeman when I grew up. On the contrary, this all changed when I got my first taste of being dressed in military uniform when I turned thirteen years old and joined the cadets. The cadets are a youth organisation for boys and girls between the ages of thirteen and eighteen, which aimed to teach cadets not only some military skills but also to make teenagers more responsible members of their communities. There was the A.C.F. (*Army Cadet Force*), associating with the British Army, the A.T.C. (*Air Training Corps*), associating with the Royal Air Force, and the Sea Cadets, associating with the Royal Navy or the C.C.F. (*Combined Cadet Force*). The latter being more associated with schools and was a combination of the A.C.F., A.T.C. and the Sea Cadets. It was not compulsory when one left the cadets that they enlisted into either of the armed services as many cadets do.

I first joined the 1966 Sqn (*Squadron*) A.T.C., which was based in Wavertree, when I was thirteen years old. However, I became bored after about nine months, and in 1984, I left that squadron to join the 2nd Signals, Royal Corps of Signals - A.C.F., which was then based in Netherley Comprehensive Secondary School. Being in the army cadets made me realize that I no longer wanted to become a policeman; thus, after I completed my Certificate of Secondary Education and Sixteen Plus examinations in June of 1987, where I attended Gateacre Community Comprehensive School, I enlisted into the Royal Corps of Signals at the age of sixteen as a junior soldier.

2

The Royal Corps of Signals - more commonly known in the British Army as the Royal Signals - depot, 11th Signal Regiment, also known as 11 Sigs, was based in Helles Barracks in Catterick Garrison, North Yorkshire. 11 Sigs was a place where adult soldiers and junior soldiers completed their basic training. Adult basic training was for nine weeks and junior basic training was for six months. Royal Signals junior leaders whose basic training was for twelve months, and apprentices completed their training at the Royal Corps of Signals Apprentice College, Harrogate. The difference between a junior soldier and a junior leader was the person's age. If one had just turned sixteen years of age when one was due to enlist into the army, then they qualified to become a junior leader.

When I got to Darlington train station, I was met by a tall, stern looking Corporal, Dave King, in number 2 dress uniform that was a matching brown trousers and tunic, and he would be one of our Troop corporals. He looked menacing as he directed me with his right hand in his black peak cap with the highly polished peak flat against his forehead resting on the bridge of his nose, to a waiting coach outside of the train station. There were already quite a few lads on the coach and when a couple more lads arrived, we made our way to camp. I kept quietly to myself on this journey as I knew there would be plenty of time to get to know my fellow recruits.

When I arrived at 8 Sigs (*8th Signal Regiment*) camp, everyone on the coach was placed into Kohima Troop. This Troop was named after the Battle of Kohima in 1944, which was a hill town in Northeast India, and, indeed, a perfect strategic position for the British Army to push into Burma. The Royal Signals provided radio comms (*communications*) for The British Army's 2nd Division, leading up to the defeat of the Japanese offensive to take control of Burma's crucial strategic position.

Even though the juniors were part of 3 Sqn, 11 Sigs, no room was to be found at Helles Barracks to accommodate our squadron, so we were billeted in Vimy Barracks, which was across the road from Helles Barracks and the home of 8 Sigs. I had many difficulties with my fitness and found the physical aspects of basic training to be a struggle.

Moreover, I was placed in jail for three days for chucking my beret at one of my Corporal's, Tony Gaston's, face because he ordered me too many press-ups to do. With much regret, I decided to leave the army half way through my six-months of basic training; although I knew I could always re-enlist in years to come if I wanted to.

On returning back home to Civvie Street, I found work in a McDonalds Hamburger Restaurant on the corner of Lord Street and Paradise Street in Liverpool City Centre, where I remained working until November of 1988. Just two days before my 18th birthday, I packed up and moved down South to Reading, Berkshire with my stepmother's nephew, who I had never met before, and did warehouse work for a computer company called International Computers Limited through an employment agency. Soon, I moved on and got a job in Burton's men's-wear with Hodes clothes concession. And after a couple of weeks, a vacancy became available within the company for a concession manager in a men's clothes shop called Concept Man in my home city of Liverpool. So, I moved back to Liverpool to fill the concession manager's position in June of 1989. I was sacked from my position of concession manager and, also from Hodes Fashions by the company's owner by telephone in August of 1989 for not reaching my weekly sale targets. I found it to be difficult and hard for me to sell the types of suits that the company was producing for the fashion conscious people of Liverpool because the suits were not trendy enough. I tried to tell the company this, but confronting them went against me. Moreover, at that particular time, it was crucial and bad to be unemployed, not just in Liverpool but other parts of the United Kingdom as well because of the recession of the mid 1980's.

On the day of being sacked, I gained the courage to ask a girl out, who I'd previously been talking to for the last few weeks, fearing embarrassment, rejection and chancing that I would never see her again. Her name was Paula, and she was a kind-hearted and an attractive 19 year old woman, who worked in the female side of the shop called 'Chelsea Girl.' When I asked her out for a drink, she accepted my offer, and we went out on that Friday night. I got a mate, Ian Sandales, to drive me in his car to pick Paula up at the bus stop outside Netherley Comprehensive School, where we arranged to meet. After picking her up, we went to the Coronation pub on the bend of Childwall Valley Road for a few drinks, and, afterwards, we went to the Grange Manor pub on

Grange Lane, Gateacre. From then on, we frequently started to go out with one another and formed a serious relationship. Still, I was unemployed and looking for some type of work.

There was not much work about in Liverpool during the year 1989. Scraps of labouring work were acquired through an employment agency, granted, I thought that it would be as good a time as any to rejoin the army. Hence, in the autumn of 1989, I made another visit to the Army Careers office to start the re-enlistment process. The Army Careers office was based in Derby Square in Liverpool City Centre and shared the same office with the Royal Navy Careers. Despite the best efforts of the recruitment Sergeant from the 1st Battalion, The King's Regiment, which was the local infantry regiment at the time, which recruits its soldiers from Liverpool and Manchester, who tried to get me to enlist into 'The King's,' I decided that I wanted to go back into the Royal Signals. This decision was not only a sentimental reason for being in the Signals cadets, but it was also a reason to prove that I did have the ability to pass the Royal Signals basic training, after a failing attempt two and a half years previously. The difference between an infantry regiment and a Corps like the Royal Signals or the Royal Engineers is that an infantry regiment tended to recruit soldiers from the county in which they're named after; on the contrary, a Corps recruits its soldiers from all over the country.

3

In February of 1990, I re-enlisted into the Royal Signals and returned to 11 Sigs in Catterick, where I'd been a Junior Soldier two and a half years previous and I went into 3 Troop, which was part of 1 Sqn. The same RQMS (*Regimental Quarter Master Sergeant Major*) was still there and in charge of the clothing stores. I remembered him from my earlier time as a junior, and he remembered me from my time in jail, for he was on duty as the Orderly Officer on one of those days. The RQMS even asked me how my dad was doing because he knew that my dad was disabled. Also, he had phoned my dad up when I was in jail and let him know that I was alright. Another shock occurred to me when one of my Troop's Corporals, Ian Holt, who I'd never met before, told me that he knew who I was and what I'd done to his roommate, Tony Gaston, back when I flung my beret at him whilst I tried for the juniors. I didn't know what to say or do and all I thought about was because of that situation, it was seemingly going to be a long time in basic training. To be fair to Corporal Holt, he did not hold the incident with his mate against me or treat me any differently to any other recruit, and we got on quite well. One time towards the end of basic training, Ian Holt informed me that he would take me into battle with him, and I took this as a compliment.

Surely, adult basic training was not quite eventful free. I somehow managed to get myself into trouble on several occasions. First off, I lost my Chit in Lieu identity card whilst I was on area cleaning, picking the rubbish up outside Barry Block, which was our accommodation adjacent to the garden of remembrance of ex-members of the Royal Signals who had died whilst still serving. Then, I immediately reported my lost card to Sergeant Snell, who was my Troop Sergeant, and he warned me for OC's, (*Officer Commanding*) orders. I went in front of my Squadron OC, Major Robinson, to be punished for losing my identity card and got fined £50. I was only in basic training for a couple of weeks, and I was already in the shit. Without a doubt, the shit really hit the fan when in the middle of basic training I punched a lad in the face down at the rifle ranges.

The lad was McErlean, a manc, from Manchester, and his partner in crime was Foster, a Yorkshire man from Leeds. They were originally in the intake before our troop and for whatever reason the pair of them got

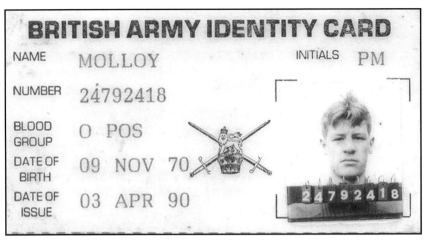

BRITISH ARMY IDENTITY CARD

NAME	MOLLOY	INITIALS	PM
NUMBER	24792418		
BLOOD GROUP	O POS		
DATE OF BIRTH	09 NOV 70		
DATE OF ISSUE	03 APR 90		

My ID Card that was issued after my chit-in-lieu, Catterick, April 1990.

'back trooped' into our troop to complete their basic training. From the moment McErlean and Foster came into my troop, the pair of them would take the piss out of me because I came from Liverpool. I had been hassle free of where I came from until these two gobshites joined my troop. They would call me a thieving Scouse bastard, a soft Scouse cunt and many more names that are malicious because I was a Scouser. The native people of Liverpool were known as Scousers. The term 'Scouse' is a name of a stew that the natives of Liverpool eat; thus, this is how we got our nickname. I took this verbal abuse for weeks and never once let it get to me until that day down at the rifle range.

Our troop had just finished firing our 9mm Model L2A3 MK4 SMG (*Sterling Machine Gun*), and we were cleaning our weapons in the range hut. The hut was made out of sturdy brick with only one way in and one way out. Inside the hut were benches, running along both sidewalls and a couple of tables ran against the back wall. I was sitting on the tables cleaning my weapon when suddenly, right out of the blue and for no reason at all, McErlean started calling me all the Scouse bastards under the sun. This was done in front of the entire troop including one of our troop Corporals, Corporal Mel Hough, but he hadn't done anything to prevent the verbal abuse against me, as it continued. Some other members of my troop were laughing at the anti Scouse comments. I was not going to tolerate it nor let it continue, so I looked up at McErlean and said to him angrily and loudly, so everyone in the hut could hear, "If you don't fucking shut up now, I'll come over there and break your fucking nose!"

McErlean looked at his mate, Foster, and sarcastically announced to the well attentive troop audience, "Typical Scouser; all talk and no action."

There were a few giggles going around the hut after McErlean made his statement. And, I knew that if I did not back up my threat to McErlean that I would continue to be verbally bullied, and not only by McErlean and Foster, but there were some others in my troop that did not like Scousers and would also fancy their chances with me. I calmly placed my SMG on the table where I was sitting, stood up abroad and steadily walked to McErlean, staring him down like a hawk stares down its prey before they kill. I didn't say a word to McErlean as I approached him. Everyone else in the hut, including Corporal Hough, stopped talking and focused their attention on what was about to happen. McErlean remained seated as I drew nearer to him, which made it very difficult for him to defend himself. Without saying a further word to McErlean, I made a fist with my right hand, pulled it back, and, then, with my full force, I drove my fist straight onto his nose, breaking it and hearing it crack. McErlean's nose started to gush blood from both his nostrils. I only hit McErlean the once, and that was all it took to shut the goby manc cunt up. Corporal Hough approached me and told me, "Get outside the hut, Molloy." Corporal Hough followed me outside and said to me, "Right Molloy, I'm warning you for orders."

Now, I was in the shit again, but because the offence I committed was more serious, I had to go in front of the CO (*Commanding Officer*), but this time I was not throwing my towel in and giving up. Instead, I would take my punishment like a man when I would be on CO's orders after my pass out parade. After this incident with McErlean, he did not give me any more verbal abuse nor did his mate, Foster. In fact, after that incident, McErlean, Foster and I became mates and not a cross word between us was said for the rest of the duration of basic training.

This time, I completed adult basic training, which was nine weeks long and involved learning skills, such as weapon handling, field craft and foot drill. I was able to meet these physical challenges of basic training this time round and passed out of basic training in Catterick to start my trade training. Paula came up to Catterick from Liverpool the night before my pass out parade to watch me pass out. Since Paula came up, I travelled back to Liverpool on the train with her. The entire troop was given one week's leave after the pass out parade before returning to Catterick and going to 8 Sigs to start their trade training except for me. I was only given the weekend off because I was on CO's orders first thing on the following Monday morning for punching McErlean and I was specifically advised not to go absent without leave; otherwise, I would even be in further trouble.

I returned back to 11 Sigs after my weekend leave to face the wrath of the CO. In the corridor just outside the CO's office of 11 Sigs RHQ (*Regimental Headquarters*), stood the RSM (*Regimental Sergeant Major*), and he told me to remove my belt and beret. This was always done before going on orders in case my punishment was jail. When the CO was ready, the RSM marched me into the CO's office at fast pace and loudly calling out the time, "Left right left right left right left!"

He gave me the command to halt just in front of the CO's desk. I remained stood in the attention position and kept my eyes firmly fixed straight ahead. The CO called out what charge I was on, which was an assault charge contrary to military law and asked me if I was going to plead guilty or not guilty. With attestation, I plead guilty, and then, the CO asked me if I wanted to accept his award. I told him that I did accept, and the CO awarded me a £200 fine. This also meant a regimental entry on my service record and for that I could kiss good bye to my Long Service and Good Conduct Medal if I wanted to make a career out of the army. The RSM ordered me to about turn, and he marched me out of the CO's office at another fast pace and a loud calling out of the time. When we were outside the CO's office, the RSM told me to replace my belt and beret, for I was now free to start my trade training at 8 Sigs. Also, he told me that he understood I was provoked in that particular situation; nevertheless, he told me that I could not go round hitting people. Oddly, this was one thing I couldn't get my head around - the army trained me to fight, and, when I did get into a fight, the army punished me.

4

Ever since joining the Royal Signal cadets in 1984, all I wanted to be was a Rad Op (*Radio Operator*). I trained for thirteen weeks as a Rad Op with 3 Sqn, 8 Sigs, which was located just across the road from 11 Sigs in Vimy Barracks. This included a week at the end of the course with Schemes Troop that involved going on exercise for a week and putting into practice everything we had learnt over the previous twelve weeks. All the combat trades, such as Rad Ops and Powerman Drivers only to name but two were in 3 Sqn. The technician trades were all part of 1 Sqn, and all the other trades like Data Telegraphist, attracting mainly women and were also known as 'handbags,' were part of 2 Sqn. The way to recognise which squadron a squaddie (*soldier*) was a member of, was distinguished by coloured nylon tabs that were worn on the epaulets. Red was for 3 Sqn, blue was for 1 Sqn and the 'handbags' in 2 Sqn wore green. Mainly, all training to be a Rad Op centered round the installation and operating of HF (*High Frequency*), and, VHF (*Very High Frequency*), vehicle mounted Clansman radio sets, types of antenna and their erection and, equally important was learning the voice procedure when talking on the sets.

About a month into my trade training my course leader, who was also a signalman, had been given the go ahead to join his new working unit, which was based in Germany. He had been placed on our course from the previous course because at the time his security clearance had not come through from the Ministry of Defence. There are times with being a Rad Op that as part of your job you have to handle equipment and material that have a 'secret' classification and therefore, security checks have to be made to enable you to be employed in that role. This left the position as course leader open. Surprisingly, I was ordered to the squadron office, for Staff Sergeant Lewington made me the new course leader. I think his decision to appoint me above anyone else was brought about with the help of Sergeant Ash who was posted to 55 (Independent) Signal Sqn, which was a Territorial Army (*TA*) unit. This unit was based at Aintree in Liverpool, where I had a brief spell in before I moved to Reading. My main duties were to ensure that the lads on the course got to their lessons on time, which was done by marching in a squad around camp between each lesson. If anyone was late or any members of the course got caught

Copland, me and Ossie cleaning our Gats during a break on
Schemes Troop exercise, July 1990.

messing about, the course leader got the bollocking. If this happened, as it did to me on a couple of occasions, then the member of the course, who dropped you in the shit, would be dealt with by giving him a punch, so that he would be certain not to fuck up again. Being the course leader was not always bad, for a course leader was always ensured a very good report to take to a new unit. In addition, the course leader was able to get me a good posting when I filled in my dream sheet.

The dream sheet was a form that I filled out in order to be posted to wherever I wanted to go on my next posting. Many lads wanted to be posted in exotic places like Hong Kong, Cyprus or Belize. And after they had completed half their trade training, they would put the names of the units that served in those exotic places on their dream sheet. All we were allotted to put on the sheet was a maximum of three different units. Then, the dream sheets would go off to Royal Signal's Manning and Records, where the clerks most probably piss themselves with laughter at the posting requests from the virgin tradesmen wanting exotic postings. Hence, the clerks gave those tradesmen a posting in the UK (*United Kingdom*), or part of BAOR (*British Army of the Rhine*) in Germany. I placed a Cyprus and two UK postings on my dream sheet.

Towards the end of our course, we were given confirmation of our new posting on a slip of paper, and I was being posted to HQ (*Head Quarters*),

Me in NBC kit whilst on Schemes Troop exercise, July 1990.

Berlin Signal Sqn. This was a dream posting, and I thought that our Staff Sergeant put in a good word for me in order to get this posting. Normally, if a soldier were a competitive swimmer in the Royal Signals, then they stood a good chance to be posted to Berlin.

I was made up with my posting, but on the 2nd of August 1990 when Saddam Hussein, the leader of Iraq, invaded Kuwait, and because of the

Me on radio shift during Schemes Troop exercise, July 1990.

invasion, Royal Signals Manning and Records then changed my posting to 3 Div (*3rd Armoured Division Headquarters and Signal Regiment*) based in Soest, Germany. My new unit was known as either 3 ADSR or 3 Div. And at the time, I didn't have a clue where about in Germany the base in Soest was located.

After trade training and driver training at 8 Sigs, I volunteered to do the 'Satisfied Soldier Scheme' at my local Army Careers office, the place where I had taken my initial army entrance test. The 'Satisfied Soldier Scheme' involved going on school visits to talk to the school leavers about how great the British Army was and that joining into the army would be a good and opportune job for them to do when they left school. In addition to going to schools, the Satisfied Soldier would also be the office tea boy in the careers office. Whilst on the Satisfied Soldier Scheme, I was paid approximately an extra £3.00 a day for expenses. After doing the 'Satisfied Soldier Scheme' routinely for two weeks, I got four weeks of well-deserved leave and enjoyed everyday of it. Afterward, I was off to 3 Div at San Sebastian Barracks in Soest, Germany, where I was posted in October of 1990.

3rd Armoured Divisional insignia arm patch.

5

I flew into R.A.F. Gutterslough from Luton Airport with British Midland and got talking to a lad, Daz Kirby. Daz was already posted to 3 Div as a Relay Op (*Radio Relay Operator*) in 1 Sqn, and he led me to our army coach, which was driven by a German civvie. On route to Soest, the coach stopped at other British Army barracks to let other soldiers return to their units, and it wasn't till early in the evening when I arrived at the 3 Div's camp. The camp was situated south of Soest in the Westfalen State of former West Germany. The nearest village, Korbecke, was just over a mile away.

The coach driver pulled up outside of the camp gates, and Daz and I grabbed our bags and left the coach. As I walked through the camp gates the first thing that I noticed to my left was an old green British Army Sherman Tank parked up on the grass as a monument to the old 3rd Infantry Division of the Second World War. To my right, opposite the Sherman Tank, was the camp's guardroom. I headed straight into the guardroom to report myself as soon as I thanked Daz for helping me out at the airport. I gave my details to the Guard Commander, a Corporal, and he would later be known to me as Gaz Tuff. Gaz told me to wait in the guardroom until someone arrived from the same squadron in which I was going to. Because I was a Rad Op, I would be joining 2 Sqn with all the other Rad Ops.

An Asian lad named Dave Ahmed, a Lance Corporal and 2 Sqn's accommodation block store man came to the guardroom to collect me, and he took me to my accommodation. My accommodation was a rectangular single storey building with three man bedrooms. The odd NCO (*None Commission Officer*), usually a Lance Corporal would share the three man rooms with two Signalmen. The accommodation block also had two single man bunks that were at both ends of the block and reserved for NCOs. Also, inside were communal showers, toilets, washrooms, a kitchen and a laundry area right in the centre of the accommodation block.

As Dave was issuing me my bedding, members of 2 Sqn sluggishly walked back into the block after finishing an exercise, and I thought I'd recognised one of the lads as he walked into the toilet. Dave showed me to my new bedroom, and told me that I would be sharing this

My bed space in our 3 man room at 3 ADSR, Soest, November 1990.

accommodation with a Lance Corporal, Wayne Coates and another signalman from Liverpool named Mick Sell, who was known to everyone as Selly. After I introduced myself to my new roommates and made my bed up, I went to look for the lad I thought I'd recognised. And, I easily tracked him down in the communal washrooms as he was cleaning his beret after coming off the exercise. He was talking to a smaller blonde haired lad I knew to be young Greenhough because he had been on the same Rad Op's course as me. Greenhough was also known as 'Greeny' to everybody and was only 17, but looked as if he should still be in school. I was almost certain he was the lad I knew when I heard is Liverpool accent. I approached him and said advertently with a loud voice, "Alright mate! Don't I know you? You were in the juniors at Catterick in Battleaxe Troop in 1987, weren't yeah? What's yeah name again?"

He looked at me with a puzzled expression on his face, replying, "Yeah. That's right. And, I know your face too…my name is Jay, Jay Craine."

"Alright mate," I said, as we shook hands.

I continued to remind Jay that I was in Kohima Troop, and that we used to talk to one another all the time because we were both from Liverpool and he was the only Scouser in his troop as well. As we got to talking, I told him that I got out, but decided to join back up again. With a quick insight, Jay remembered that we used to talk together, and that we both

Jay Craine and me on Remembrance Sunday, Soest, November 1990.

sat our army entrance test together at the Army Careers Office in Liverpool. Back then was the first time Jay and I met each other. Although Jay hadn't yet been promoted and was still a Signalman, knowing another lad from back home, I was glad that I was acquisitioned to that particular accommodation, I was thinking whilst falling off asleep.

The following morning, I went down to 2 Sqn. offices with Selly. Their

Mick Sell 'bulling' his boots for Remembrance Sunday,
Soest, November 1990.

Jay Craine writing a rather long letter home to his girlfriend,
Soest, November 1990.

offices were situated on the other side of the road and on the other side
of the football pitch outside camp. The squadron office was part of an old
prison, which still had all of its prison cells, but they were now converted
and used to store military equipment. I stood to attention in the corridor
with my heels together, my arms straight down each side of my body and
locked in tight with my shoulders back and my head held up with my
neck at the back of my highly starched shirt collar. I introduced myself
to the SSM (*Squadron Sergeant Major*), named Billy Haslam. SSM Billy
Haslam told me to take myself to see Staff Sergeant Beattie in Oscar
Troop and to let Staff Sergeant Beattie know that I was joining his troop.
Oscar Troop's office was only a few yards down the corridor from the
SSM's office. I stood to attention at the open door of Oscar Troop's office
and asked for Staff Sergeant Beattie. A husky and burly man with dark
hair, a Northern Irishman with a well-groomed moustache informed me
that he was the person that I was looking for. I explained to him that I had
just arrived at 3 Div the night previous, and that I was a new Rad Op.
Staff Sergeant Beattie welcomed me to the troop and asked one of the
troop Sergeants, Sergeant Neaves, to take me to the garages, where the
rest of the troop were working on their vehicles, so he could introduce
me to the troop. On our way to the garages, Sergeant Neaves gave me
some advice with being the new kid on the block. He wisely said to me,

Mick Sell making out an inventory for his MFO box,
Soest, December 1990.

"Right, Molloy. The best thing for you to do for the next six months is to keep your mouth shut and keep your eyes and ears open. After that period of time has past, then you can open your mouth. Do you understand?"

"Yes Sergeant." I nervously replied, wandering what the fuck I'd let myself into.

When we arrived at the garages, I saw the entire troop's 436 tracked armoured radio vehicles all parked up. Sergeant Neaves introduced me to another Signalman, 'Spud' Hewitt. Sergeant Neaves told Spud that I would be on his vehicle and for Spud to show me around and to show me the ropes.

"Okay Sarge," Spud eagerly answered.

Spud asked me if I had been to RHQ, to let them know that I had arrived. I told him that I had not, so another Signalman, Daz Garton, who I recognised from 8 Sigs, said he would take me to RHQ to get sorted out with any documentation. I think Daz's offer to assist me was more to do with not bothering to want to work than to be friendly and helpful.

When Daz and I got to RHQ, I introduced myself to a clerk, who was a Corporal, and he sat behind the counter. The clerk checked my details, and, then, he informed me that I was not expected at 3 Div until the 5th of November. Because I wasn't expected there yet, I asked the clerk if it would then be possible for me to go back home for some more leave and

Jay Craine and Mick Sell raving in my room,
Soest, December 1990.

turn back up the following month. Grinning, the clerk laughed and answered me with a trite remark, "No chance."

I was a bit disappointed at the clerk's audacity because I was already missing Paula after one day; nevertheless, once I had filled in all the necessary documentation in RHQ, I went with Daz back down to the garages and squadron stores to be issued with 1958 pattern webbing. I was surprised to see Dave King, who was now a Staff Sergeant and the squadron's QM (*Quarter Master*). With Dave King being the squadron's QM, he was in charge of the squadron stores from bedding to webbing, which meant we would address him as 'Q' rather than 'Staff'. I thought he would give me a bit of a rough ride because of what I'd done to his mate, Tony Gaston, back when I was in the juniors. Dave King prevented Tony Gaston from punching me by grabbing his right arm after I chucked my beret in Tony's face. Dave King was also surprised to see me, and he shook my hand and welcomed me to the squadron. Dave King informed me that there were a few lads from Kohima Troop at 3 Div that I would know, lest he told me that Tony Gaston was also in Soest, but he was posted at 206 Signal Sqn. at Salamanca Barracks, which was a couple of miles away from our camp.

It was not clear towards the end of November 1990 whether I was going to the Persian Gulf or not because on numerous occasions I was

Young Greenhough doing a bit of last minute washing in the block,
Soest, December 1990.

told by my troop Staff Sergeant that I would not be going out there, but,
on other occasions, he told me I was. There is a saying in the army used
for this type of situation, 'On the bus off the bus.' And, it happens quite
frequently in the British Army.

Going to war wasn't bothersome to me, for I wanted to go to the Gulf
with my mates and not miss out on anything. Finally, at the end of
November 1990, it was confirmed that I was going on *Op Granby*
(*Operation Granby*).

Op Granby was the British Army's encoded name for the 'Desert
Storm' war against Iraq and its dictator, Saddam Hussein and his
wickedly evil Regime in the Persian Gulf. I would be attached to 1 Sqn.
as a Trunk Node's recce (*reconnaissance*) driver and Rad Op. Trunk
Node is the comms name of our troop and is normally referred to as a
Node. In addition, Nodes provide static UHF (*Ultra High Frequency*) and
SHF (*Super High Frequency*) comms through directional antennas
mounted on the back of Bedford's and were able to be deployed at
anytime, in a similar way of a mobile telephone exchange. I saw my
name, along with everyone else's name from my squadron, on the
squadron's notice board. Suddenly, it was ratified. And, I turned away
from the notice board, jumped up, punching the air and screamed, "Yes!"

This was sensational news, arousing excitement in me. And, now, I was satisfied of not being left behind to guard the camp whilst everyone else went off to war. Most of my fellow troop members were being sent to 204 Signal Sqn, which were part of 4 Brigade (*4th Armoured Brigade*), to boost up that squadrons numbers, so they could help interdict and regulate Saddam Hussein's malicious hostilities. No one likes to be left behind to do rear details of the camp, such as guard duties and maintaining the vehicles that were left behind.

Mick Sell and me sporting our Gulf haircuts,
Soest, December 1990.

6

The medical process for preparing us for the Gulf started towards the end of November 1990. We had to pay a visit to the medical centre at Salamanca Barracks, which was the home of 6 Brigade (*6th Armoured Brigade*) and 206 Signal Sqn, because our camp did not have its own medical centre. We had our medicals there to see if we were fit for operational service, and I was passed as fully fit. I also had to receive a cocktail of injections that were supposed to prevent me catching any nasty diseases. Consequently, I had had a reaction to the Cholera injection that I received when I got back up to my own camp. I was walking by the garages as I began to feel dizzy, and with a quirk, I collapsed in convulsions with my body shaking uncontrollably. This lasted for a few minutes, and, then, I was able to pick myself up off the floor. I still felt a bit feverish, but with not long to final parade I soldiered on. After my evening meal, the hot flushes came back, and my body started shaking again, and, therefore, I put myself to bed early with being on guard the following day. I hoped that in the morning all of the ailments I had gotten would be gone. In the morning I got up late; thus, I was late for guard and could have gotten into deep shit for not turning up for duty on time. But, I explained to the guard commander how I had a reaction to the Cholera injection the day before, and he didn't report me. Still, I was not feeling my usual one hundred percent when I turned up for guard, but as the day drew on my body returned to normal.

In the second week of December 1990, every soldier from 1 Sqn, who were being deployed on *Op Granby*, needed to go to the British Army's training camp at Senelager, which was near Paderborn, Germany, for the necessitated pre-Gulf War training was expedited at that location before their send off. This training was also in conjunction with the daily training that we had been receiving in camp ever since we were informed that we would be going to the Gulf. The pre-Gulf War training was not just for members of our squadron, but, also, for every member of the British Army who was being deployed on *Op Granby*. I noticed other cap badges at Senelager, such as the R.C.T. (Royal Corps of Transport) and Artillery (*Royal Artillery*). The training lasted for three days and consisted of an array of range work, firing our personal weapons, which were the 7.62mm L1A1 SLR (*Self-Loading Rifle*), along with the

7.62mm LMG (*Light Machine Gun*). The LMG would be used for air defence. You would have to be one hell of a shot to shoot down an Iraqi MiG flying at a speed of 600 miles per hour at low level with a LMG. Apart from firing our weapons of a day, we also needed to complete a night shoot. That was an insight, and we all hoped that the Iraqis didn't attack us at night because hardly anyone of us managed to hit the target. The other weapons we needed to be trained on were the L2A2 Hand Grenade and the M72 66mm Light Anti-Tank Weapon. The lads always referred to the latter as the '66.' This was the first time I had ever thrown a hand grenade and fired the '66,' which I'd really looked forward to.

First, the NCO in charge of the grenade range gave our group a quick insight to the grenade and an insight on how to throw it too. When I stepped up to the firing point, the NCO instructed me first on how to prime the grenade by screwing the fuse into the top of the grenade. I must admit that I was shitting myself at this point just in case I made a mistake and both the NCO and I had parts of us all over the grenade range.

The fuse screwed in smoothly and I held the grenade in my right hand. Then, I was told by the NCO to place my left index finger in the ring of the grenade pin whilst drawing the grenade up to my chest, which I eagerly did. Next, the NCO instructed me to keep a firm hold of the handle when I pulled the pin out. Whilst the handle was depressed the grenade would not go off, but my arse was still twitching just in case I had a dodgy fuse. After that, the NCO explained that I needed to pull my right arm back and lob the grenade over my arm whilst screaming the warning, Grenade. I took on board in my head what the NCO had just told me, and as I lobbed the grenade as far as possible, I screamed at the top of my voice "Grenade."

Both the NCO and I ducked for cover behind the sandbags and approximately four seconds later a dull boom was heard when the grenade exploded. I was relieved to still be in one piece and looked forward to firing the 66.

When our group reached the anti-tank range, where we would be firing the 66, the NCO in charge of this range also went through the specifications of the weapon. The main specifications were that the 66 was a single shot and discard weapon with an effective range of up to 500 meters and could penetrate armour in excess of 650mm thick. A safety distance of at least 20 meters was needed at the rear of the weapon when firing. When the 66 was extended, the sights automatically popped up. I was very excited to get the opportunity to play with this weapon because when in a Corps it is very rare that a soldier got to fire the 66. There were a couple of old rusty armoured vehicles on the range in front of me that looked as if they had been well blown up by easily excited soldiers like me. The NCO pointed out to me the armoured vehicle I was to fire at, which was about 200m in front of me. I pulled the 66 out to extend it and ready it to fire, and, then, I placed it on my right shoulder and looked at the target through the sights. When the 200m line of the sight was lined up with the armoured vehicle, I squeezed the trigger, which was on top of the weapon, and the weapon made a whooshing sound when the rocket was fired. As I was watching the rocket head towards the target, the NCO pulled me down behind the firing point for safety reasons. Before I went for cover, I did manage to see that the shot failed to hit the target as the rocket fell just short of it. I hoped that I did not have to use this weapon in real combat.

The three-day training was not all about weapons. We had lectures on NBC (*Nuclear, Biological and Chemical*) warfare. More lectures were on hygiene in the field by members of the RAMC (*Royal Army Medical Corps*) as well. We were also informed about what diseases we could possibly catch in the Middle East if our personal hygiene was not spot on. Another lecture was on the wild animals that we could have encounter in the desert. Pictures of these animals and the damage they could cause to humans were projected on to a screen via an OHP (*Over Head Projector*).

The scariest animal for most of the lads and I was the Camel Spider because the WO II (*Warrant Officer*) from the RAMC, who was giving the lecture, informed us that this creature was highly venomous. Moreover, the creature's venom contained an anaesthetic that numbed their victims while the creature ate away at its prey. The WO II showed us the damage that these creatures did, and it appeared to be across between a spider and a scorpion, could do to flesh. All of this was shown to us by a projection on a screen of a picture of a camel with part of its flesh eaten away. When I saw the damage caused by the camel spider it sent shivers down my spine, and I knew I would have to keep my wits about me when I went into the desert.

Whilst I was doing my pre Gulf War training, I came across a lad, Moore, who I had met when we both went to Sutton Coldfield, and we had a chat for a few minutes to see how each one of us was getting on.

Sutton Coldfield was the British Army's camp just outside Birmingham in the Midlands, and that is were every prospective recruit had to go to do their fitness tests, final aptitude tests and final interview and pass before being offered a place in an infantry regiment or corps that they chose. Moore was from Formby, which is quite an affluent area of Merseyside, and he had gone on to join the Artillery. We shook hands and wished each other all the best for our time in the Gulf. And after that, we never saw each other again.

When we returned back to Soest from our three day pre Gulf War training, we were all informed that we would be given five days leave before leaving for Saudi Arabia on the 21st of December 1990. All the lads were made up with this news, as we did not expect to receive any leave before departing to the Gulf.

4th Armoured Brigade insignia arm patch, Gulf War, 1991.

7

Once we were told to fall out, everyone raced to their respective accommodation blocks to pack their clothes for a few days leave. A lot of us also cleared out the NAAFI (*Navy Army Air Force Institute*) shop with beer and cigarettes for the long journey home to the UK. I took my medium size Head sports bag partly filled with clothes, and in my 100 litre capacity green Breghaus Vulcan II Bergen where I placed 5 boxes of 20 bottled Lagers, and in the Bergen's side pouches were a dozen loose bottles of Grolsch lager, which saw me through my 5 days leave. Scouse Robbo, a plastic Scouser from Hale Village just outside Liverpool, who was also another Rad Op, and also attached to 1 Sqn doing the same job as me but in another troop managed to bum a lift with Andy in his car. Andy was a Relay Lance Corporal from my new adopted troop in 1 Sqn. Andy wasn't a big lad, small and slim and spoke with a soft Brummie accent with him coming from Birmingham. Andy would only take Scouse Robbo and me as far as Birmingham New Street train station, as Andy lived in Birmingham.

There was a mass exudes from the camp by all the singlelies (*single soldiers*) lads heading back to the UK. We raced to Calais to catch our ferry to Dover via a small German village called Wankum, which was very close to the German and Belgium border to refuel. This was the last place in Germany where Andy could use his tax-free fuel coupons. We had a couple of piss stops on our way to the seaport because Scouse Robbo and I had been drinking our lager ever since we left camp. The journey to Calais took us about 5 hours, and we managed to make the ferry that sailed just after midnight.

When Andy parked the car on the ferry we all headed straight for the bar. There were even more lads from our squadron already in the bar including our troop OC, Lieutenant Naden, waiting for the bar to open. Lieutenant Naden was in his early twenties, but looked not long out of secondary school. He spoke with a posh English accent, which meant he must come from a well-to-do family. When we talked to Lieutenant Naden, who was not that much older than ourselves, we did not call him sir as we were not back in camp plus for security reasons with the ferry being full of civilians and anyone of them could have been a member of the IRA (*Irish Republican Army*), and specifically for security reasons we did not want to single the young lad out as being an officer. There had been many IRA attacks in the past on British military personnel serving in Germany. His first name was Andy, and for the duration of the ferry crossing that is what we called him. All the lads were very high spirited on the 75 minute ferry crossing to Dover just getting pissed and having a good laugh with each other because there was no point in trying to catch some sleep, although we did try to catch a few winks.

Scouse Robbo and I managed to get about an hours sleep in the back of Andy's car on our third leg of the journey, which was from Dover Channel Port to Birmingham New Street train station. When we got to the station, Andy dropped us off at about six o'clock in the morning, but there were no direct trains to Liverpool for a couple of hours, so the pair of us jumped a train to Stafford, where we changed trains to get to Manchester Piccadilly, and then we got our final train to Liverpool Lime Street. It was on the train to Manchester Piccadilly at around seven-thirty in the morning that I decided to lift the lid off my Bergen and have a liquid breakfast. I passed Scouse Robbo a bottle of lager and we started to drink again. I did offer a lager to the civvies around me, but they declined my kind offer. By the time the train pulled into Manchester Piccadilly, which was not long after eight o'clock in the morning, we were both feeling slightly pissed again.

I looked at the timetable to find out what time the train was due into Liverpool Lime Street, and we had 45 minutes to wait. Therefore, Scouse Robbo delved into his sports bag and pulled out two bottles of Grolsch lager, and we continued with our liquid breakfast.

The platform, where we were both waiting for the Liverpool train, started to fill up with a mass of passengers, as Scouse Robbo and I were both becoming more and more rowdy as we consumed more and more lager. A British Transport policeman approached the pair of us an instructed us to behave ourselves. The policeman looked down at our bags and asked, "Where are you from?"

I knew exactly what the policeman meant, but I sarcastically replied, "Liverpool."

The policeman was not too happy with my reply; as a result, with a bit more assertiveness in his voice, he once again demanded to know where we were from, so he asked the question again, "As if I couldn't tell, but where have you just come from?"

Without slurring my words to prevent myself from facing the

possibility of being arrested for D 'n' D (*drunken and disorderly*), I arrogantly replied, "We've just come from Germany, and we're off to the Gulf in five days."

"Okay lads. I understand you've got a difficult job to do, but can you keep it down a bit for us," he instructed us before walking away.

Scouse Robbo and I started laughing at the policeman, as he knew there was no point in pursuing the matter any further. Our bottles were just about empty, so I looked around the platform and amongst the masses of commuters and noticed a group of three girls in their teens that looked like they were students, and I thought I could have a laugh with them.

Once I recharged our bottles of lager, I nudged Scouse Robbo and said, "Hey Robbo, see those birds over there? They've lost that loving feeling."

Scouse Robbo realised what I was getting at and nervously replied "No they haven't."

"Oh, yes they have," I said as we were approaching the group of girls.

When we got nearer, we stopped a couple of feet in front of them, dropped down on one knee and broke into the first verse and chorus of *You've Lost That Loving Feeling*, imitating what Tom Cruse did to Kelly McGillis in the 1986 blockbuster film *Top Gun.* Our singing was load and well out of tune, but it made all of the commuters stop what they were doing like reading a paper, and they focused their attention on us two pissed up squaddies embarrassing three girls. The girls did not know what to do about us singing to them. They giggled and their cheeks reddened with embarrassment and held their heads in their hands whilst looking at the floor. When we had finished our terrible rendition of one of the best songs sung by *The Righteous Brothers*, the girls laughed along with a load of commuters. Scouse Robbo offered them all a bottle of lager, but they thought it was too early and declined his offer. We chatted with the girls about being in the army and we were going to try and impress them until our train arrived. We said our goodbyes and the girls wished us both luck for our forth-coming uncertain adventure to the Gulf.

When we got on the train, we noticed another British Army travel bag, so the both of us went through the train carriages searching for the owner of the army travel bag. When we were walking back to our seats, we noticed the familiar drunken figure of young Greeny slumped on the table trying to sleep. Scouse Robbo woke him up by laughing and saying to him while shoving a bottle of lager into his hand, "Hey, Greeny, wake up. You've missed your stop, and you're on yeah way to Liverpool."

"Fuck it," Greeny mumbled still half a sleep and then took a swig of his bottle of lager.

I also bumped into an old school mate on the train, Graham Nolan, and we chatted over our old school days and who we were still in contact with from school. When the train arrived at Liverpool Lime Street, I said good-bye to Graham and staggered along the platform with my fellow drunken brothers in arms, Scouse Robbo and Greeny. I said good-bye to Scouse Robbo and Greeny as they went to check for the next departing train to Manchester, and I made my way to Paula's work.

The five days leave was mostly spent going out with my mates and Paula. All I wanted to do whilst on this leave was to be with Paula and make love to her all the time just in case I did die in battle, at least I would have died having had sex for the last time. However, that didn't go to plan with what Paula told me when we were in bed about to make love. She told me that she had gone to an abortion clinic with her mother and had an abortion. I did not know she was even pregnant. I knew before I left the UK to go on my posting to Germany that she had not started her period, however, when I phoned Paula from Germany she informed me that her periods had started again. I did not really feel anything at the time, for I was more concerned on how Paula was feeling. The moment was lost, and not just for that night but also for every night that I was home, Paula, and I never made love.

At the end of my leave, Paula came to Liverpool Lime Street train station with me to see me off. We held each other tight, and I gave her a long lingering kiss before I boarded the train. Then, my train pulled out of the station to make its way to Birmingham New Street train station, where I would be meeting up with Scouse Robbo and Andy to make our way back to Germany. And, we all departed on our uncertain future. We did not know whether we would be leaving Iraq on an aeroplane sitting in a seat or travelling in the hull of that aeroplane in a body bag.

8

On the 20th of December 1990, mostly every junior rank member of 1 Sqn gathered in the NAAFI bar for a righteous send-off. The night before leaving for the parade and the war was beyond crazy. I don't know what possessed me to drink so much, but it was surely painful the next day. The thoughts, 'I've got to get up,' rung round in my head until I thought I was going to be sick. The room spun, the bed spun, and I spun until the clock struck 08.00. "Shit, the parade," I thought in the recesses of my hung over mind.

The padre's service of good luck and don't get killed was before the parade took place at half past eight, and all personnel were to attend. Therefore, I dragged my battered body out of bed, and, somehow, I got dressed into my un-pressed uniform that day, which sat in a pile in the corner of the room, where it had been since the previous day's duty. The effort I made to move the few hundred yards to the gym was the most painful effort I had ever made so far in life. My eyes stung, and my breath smelt like something had crawled into my mouth in the night and died. The gym and its occupants all looked the same way that I felt, hung over and scramble minded.

The gym was filled with lines of plastic chairs, and the chairs were filled with zombie-like figures all muttering. So, I took it that we were all waiting for the padre and his praise to God. To our great disillusionment, the padre turned up.

'Please, let it be quick,' I thought to myself.

No one would survive the onslaught of the padre. Never mind the Iraqi's, if the padre had a full-blown service in mind, we'd all be sitting in the gym trying to stay awake while the padre preached to us before we went off to war. Mostly, all of the lads, including the higher ranked officers, were hung over and didn't want to sit through a long drawn out sermon. As I looked round at my brothers in arms, all eyes gazed intoxicated and looking upwardly towards the ceiling. We all listened to the padre, as the padre talked of an old friend of his and somehow related his friend's situation to our pending fate in the Persian Gulf; however, I didn't pay much attention to what he was saying, as I was more interested in wanting my body to return back to normal. We had short prayers for those already in the Gulf and Northern Ireland with a minute of silence at the end. I forced my semi-drunken body off of the chair and towards the exit. Surprisingly, we were all given a small Bible. Ah, I thought, the army have finally listened to the soldier in the field and realised three sheets of coarse toilet paper in a 24 hour ration pack just don't do the job. The faces of those around me all told different stories, some scared, some thrilled, some excited, but my only thoughts were getting to the phone to call Paula. All I thought about was Paula, but the gym echoed to a numbed silence as the padre left.

Afterwards, the RSM broke the silence with his dulcet tones, ordering us to our feet, which we did with great difficulty still hung-over. The day for most of us would be long as we were given our passports, ID discs and associated documents, such as an identity card called a F/Ident/189, which had my name, rank, number and date of birth written twice in ink on it just in case I was captured and I would have to give the bottom copy to my captives. This document had to be issued in compliance with the provisions of Article 17 of Geneva (POW) Convention, 1949. This process involved endless signing and re-signing. Each troop, assembled with their personal kit of more combat uniforms, socks, underpants and any other bits of clothing or equipment was packed into military travel bags, 1958 pattern webbing and Bergen's behind the Senior NCOs ready for the arrival of the Bedford 4 ton trucks, which were used to transport troops and equipment. The Bedfords hauled the personal kit to Hannover International Airport where our kit would be loaded onto our R.A.F flight to Al Jubayl, Saudi Arabia.

The exception was my personal weapon, the SLR, or otherwise known as a Gat by every member of the Royal Signals. My Gat would travel with me, wrapped in Hessian, in the hull of the aircraft. Now, we stood there waiting for the imminent arrival of the trucks, worrying if we packed those essentials because nothing could be attached to the outside of our kit. The Bedford's arrived, and we were all called forward by the MCO (*Movement Control Officer*) in order of rank to check our ID cards and weigh and stow our kit, which always began with the troop's officers, SNCO's, JNCO's and, lastly, the Toms. The kit, according to rank, either got placed neatly or like mine and most of the others in the troop catapulted like a bundle of rags into the back of the Bedford. While we waved bye-bye to our kit, we were stood down, and once again I thought of the phone and Paula; nonetheless, my hopes dashed because with the immortal wisdom of the British Army we were soon off to war.

Still, like the children we once were, we had to go and clean up our rooms and finish off packing our personal kit that was going to stay behind into MFO (*Military Freight Overseas*) boxes that would be stored in a secure room in the barrack block. In the event of coming back from Iraq in a body bag our next of kin would be given our MFO boxes, so we were instructed by our SSM not leave any embarrassing items or material like pornography in the MFO boxes.

This meant for a lot of the lads throwing away their collection of German pornographic video films that had been collected whilst being in Soest. It would not have been nice for a mother thinking that her little

F/Ident/189

If you are captured you are required, under the provisions of Article 17 of the Prisoner of War Convention, 1949, to give your captors the information set out below so that your capture may be reported to your next-of-kin. When you are interrogated, but not before, tear off the duplicate portion and give it to the interrogator. GIVE NO OTHER INFORMATION. *Once this card has been issued to you you must carry it upon you at all times.* In your own interest you must ensure that the particulars of your rank are kept up to date.

(Fill in your particulars in BLOCK LETTERS)

BRITISH FORCES IDENTITY CARD

(Issued in compliance with the provisions of Article 17 of Geneva (POW) Convention, 1949)

SERVICE NUMBER 24792418 RANK SIG

SURNAME MOLLOY

CHRISTIAN/ FORE NAME(s) PETER MICHAEL

DATE OF BIRTH 9 11 70

- -

BRITISH FORCES IDENTITY CARD

(Issued in compliance with the provisions of Article 17 of Geneva (POW) Convention, 1949)

(DUPLICATE)

SERVICE NUMBER 24792418 RANK SIG

SURNAME MOLLOY

CHRISTIAN/ FORE NAME(s) PETER MICHAEL

DATE OF BIRTH 9 11 70

St.S.   S50717

Fident 189, just in case I was captured.

Johnny was a respectable proud squaddie, and then, when she opened his MFO boxes, realising he was a sexual deviant and there were many of them in the British Army. Meanwhile, off to the bar we went for our last night to eat, drink and party before we headed to an uncertain future.

Once again, the entire singlelies of 1 Sqn and the single WRACs (*Women's Royal Army Corps*) of the regiment converged on the NAAFI bar. The bar, about twenty-five feet wide with table and chairs running along both sides, sat in a rectangular shaped room with high ceilings and the bar was at one end and the dance floor was eighty feet away at the other end of the room. This was the bar where every NIG (*New in Germany*) squaddie took their regimental initiation to become an accepted member of the regiment. The initiation consisted of a member of the troop that the NIG belonged to going around the bar with an empty pint glass and asking everyone in the bar to put some money in it. Then, the person who collected the money would take the contents and the glass to the bar and ask the barmaid for a top shelf in the glass. A top shelf was a shot of every spirit that was on optics literally on the top shelf. Sometimes, crisps or eggs would be added to the head banging cocktail. Once the drink had been poured, the NIG, sometimes there was more than one NIG like on my initiation, had to stand on a chair in the middle of the dance floor whilst everyone in the bar would count down from ten. The NIG needed to drink as much as he could without spilling a drop before the count reached one. If there was anything left in the glass at the end of the count, the NIG had to pour the contents over his head. And, everyone would cheer, for the NIG became an accepted member of the regiment.

It was about 8:00pm before the bar's patrons began to reach their normal state of drunken depravity. Finally, I got to slip away to phone Paula, and this was the last opportunity I had to talk to her before the other lads realized I disappeared. Eventually, when I got through on the phone, Paula did not say much, for the phone was in the living room and her parents were home. We exchanged our love for each other and said our goodbyes. Paula seemed brave as I said, "See yeah."

Saying goodbye left me feeling deeply empty inside. I felt like I would never see her again. Tears rolled slowly down my cheeks, as I replaced the handset, and, then, I wiped them away. I was going to miss Paula very much; moreover, I didn't know if I'd ever see her again. I dried my eyes and joined the almighty pissed up craziness that marked our last night of freedom and normality in Germany. The Place that the regiment had been based during the 'Cold War' with Russia and the rest of the Warsaw Pact countries, which was now ending with the start of the fall of the Communism and the Berlin Wall on 9th November 1989.

When I returned to the bar, the atmosphere was electrically ecstatic. One of the chefs, who looked like Plug from the children's Beano comic, ran around the bar chasing his beret as it was being thrown from one person to the other. Everybody laughed except the chef. This man was not a happy man, and he reminded me of a raging bull chasing around a china shop with his nostrils flaring, crashing into tables and chairs, knocking them askew and wrecking the bar. I sat in the bar, laughing, looking on and drinking my cans of Stone's bitter one after another.

Even with all of the fun going on in the bar, I still thought about my near past life and my near future life and what lie ahead. Thinking about the war I was being sent off to and not having the real reason why we were at war in the first place, I reached into my pocket, pulled out my Bible that the padre had given to me, thumbed through the pages, and I came across the Book of Revelation. One of the many passages, which caught my imagination most and stayed with me for along time, began with, "The Persian Gulf would be a sea of flames and the survivors of the war would burn to death."

The words fire and brimstone stuck in my head, knowing that I was off to engage in the war in the Persian Gulf with the rest of the British Army and our allies. The Persian Gulf was where I would be in the next twenty-four hours. 'Shit, Have I lost my bottle,' I thought as my arse started to twitch. And after that night, only a small number of lads would be left behind on rear details to ensure the smooth running of the barracks.

The war against Iraq was going to be my reality; after all, this was the alternative to the dole queue. I finished my last cans of Stone's bitter before leaving the others who carried on and enjoyed their last taste of alcohol. Our taste buds would never be the same again for some time.

Once again, we made our way to the gym, but tonight without the helpless and intoxicated effort from the previous morning. I didn't know when I would see or talk to Paula again, for in the gym was our last night of sanity from normal army life. As the evening drew upon us, I entered the gym, and bodies had begun to lie up in their doss bags (*sleeping bags*). I curled up in my doss bag, and all that was left was the crescendo of snoring bodies echoing all around me. I lay in the corner while thoughts saturated my mind of Paula; the times we walked around the Albert Dock underneath the walkway on a Sunday during the nice sunny days and even the brisk rainy days. As I drifted off to sleep, I was concerned if I would come back from the Gulf War a different person.

9

On a dark and rainy Friday morning, most of us awoke very slowly at an early 3:00am, some quicker than others. As usual, moans and groans of agony filled the room from drinking the night before, and the hangover figures suddenly became aware of what was going to happen on that particular day.

The show had begun for those of us sober enough to appreciate what would happen next. Drunken bodies rose up and fell down, and for those who were stupid enough to undress for bed were either searching endlessly for their combats (*combat trousers*), and the ones who did have their combats preceded and struggled to put them on back to front, one leg at a time, and some were able to put them on correctly. Eventually, all were dressed. The melee of drunken bodies now suitably dressed and followed the wise to breakfast, which had been booked early for us, due to the events of the coming day.

Still, the cookhouse was shrouded in spooky darkness, but there was a hive of activity, as the cooks drank during the night. The slop jockeys was the army's nickname for a chef because of the slops they served up to squaddies, and they looked as rough as the breakfast they helped to prepare for us. One of the slop jockeys noticed the queue outside the cookhouse getting bigger, so when the breakfast was ready he turned the lights on and unlocked the cookhouse doors. We threw ourselves into the ordeal, which was breakfast while some of the other lads appeared quite full of themselves to a round of applause, for there was no doubt that they disappeared with one of the many WRAC personnel, during the previous evening, saying their goodbyes; the lucky bastards. The noisy applause quickly healed and ceased as prompt as it abruptly started when the CO entered the cookhouse.

The CO wandered around the room from table to table shaking hands with individuals like we were part of some forlorn hope. He wasn't a bad bloke I supposed, for one he cared. The one thing that got to him above all was the fact that he would not be coming with us because we were not going to the Gulf as a single unit, but attached to 1 Div (*1st Armoured Division Headquarters and Signal Regiment*), and they had their own CO. The coaches that started us off on our journey were waiting on the drill square. Our destination to begin with was Hanover International

Airport. Those who were married or had girl friends locally waved them goodbye as we left the camp and left Soest. This could well be the last time I would ever see this camp again, but I thought to myself that that might not be a bad thing.

Even though the camp was shit, it was not all that bad in Soest. Furthermore, one of the best nights I ever had here was when the members of 2 Sqn a few weeks previous had a big bar room brawl with members of the Royal Jocks (*The Royal Scots (The Royal Regiment)*) in a German pub in the centre of Soest that was mainly frequented by off duty squaddies called the *Big Ben*. Members of the Royal Jocks, who were based in a town call Werl, which was about 20 minutes away from our camp, attacked one of our lads, Lavs, a Jock himself. He was attacked in Soest because he was a Scotsman in an English regiment. Members of the Royal Jocks sometimes ventured into Soest for an evening on the piss, so we agreed to pay them a visit.

The night started with all the lads who were up for it unofficially parading in the NAAFI bar at 7pm. We fuelled ourselves up on the cheap NAAFI beer for a couple of hours before taking a taxi to the *Big Ben*. I jumped in a taxi with Martin Yates, from Manchester, and we were the first to arrive at the pub. Inside the pub, the actual bar was in the centre of the room with seating areas all round the edges of the pub in the form of benches facing one another separated by a table in-between. We looked around the pub and noticed around half a dozen Royal Jocks sitting down having a drink. Martin told me to come with him and we would start it with them. I asked Martin if we should have waited until the rest of our guys turned up, but he was apt and eagerly ready for it now.

We approached the table where the Royal Jocks were sitting, and Martin asked them if they were from the Royal Jocks and as soon as one of the told Martin he was, Martin gave him a jaw breaking right hook to his face. Then, I punched one of the Royal Jocks in the face and all hell broke loose. We did not see the gang of Royal Jocks standing at the bar, and they jumped on the pair of us and started throwing stout and unbearable punches into our bodies and faces. I thought we were done for, until I felt someone prodding my back, and, then, I heard a familiar voice. It was Selly's voice. He didn't know it was me getting a hiding by a couple of Royal Jocks, and he said to me, "Are you English?"

I screamed back at him, "It's fucking me, Mick, Molly. Get the fuckers off me."

Selly and a load more lads from our squadron had just turned up in taxis, walked into the pub and started fighting with the Royal Jocks. There were bar stools being thrown at the Royal Jocks by our lads; in addition, more of our lads were running the length of the bar and jumping onto groups of Royal Jocks just turning up. Lads were getting booted in the head, bottles and glasses being thrown at each group, and the barmaid was screaming in a panicked state. People who were not involved rapidly dispersed from this little riot, which lasted about 20 minutes before British MP's (*Military Police*) and German Polizie turned up to quell the riot with their German Shepherd dogs. The Polizie let the dogs off their leads, and the dogs ran round the pub barking and growling. At this point, everyone who was fighting suddenly stopped, and it was a free for all to make good our escape. I luckily escaped because I joined in with a group who were trying to get out of the pub at the same time we all barged the front door to the pub pushing the MPs and Polizie out of the way, so we were able to escape down one of the side streets before getting a taxi back to camp. That was a good night, we battered the Royal Jocks and they never came back. Reflecting back on that night whilst sitting on the coach, made me imagine the horrid and unpleasant images waiting for us in Iraq.

As all the coaches pulled into pre-arranged bays at the rear of the airport, we off-loaded our kit and began a very long wait for our even longer flight. It was 8:30am; the weather was as regular and as predictable as it was back home, wet, cold and miserable with the only difference being that it was a lot cleaner in Germany. The room, where we waited, was large enough to hold us all, but it was bleak, frigid and bitterly cold. Bodies huddled around the few heaters that still worked. The biggest consolation was the Sally bash wagon from the Salvation Army was suppressed and tucked away in the corner with its hot tea and sandwiches.

Meanwhile, the R.A.F. movement controllers gave us a lecture on our forthcoming journey to Saudi (*Saudi Arabia*) and a pamphlet entitled 'The Gulf Crisis.' Our plane finally arrived, an R.A.F. Lockheed Tri-Star. The Tri-Star doesn't quite come in the same primary category as the world's favourite airline. There were no drop-dead gorgeous airhostesses waiting on us, and there wasn't much said about the little bit of shabbily prepared food either, for it would not have filled up an ant. As with the

Boarding the RAF Tristar at Hanover airport, 21st December 1990.

British government, no expense spared. We began to board with the smokers going first followed by us non-smokers, in the same way as if we were going on our holidays to a Mediterranean country like Spain.

When I finally got on board, I clambered over two officers to reach the seat by the window. As the flight went on, we flew high over top the Italian snow-covered Alps, and everyone leaned over towards the windows and tried to take a snapshot. I quickly took a couple pictures, and, then, I glanced out of the small window, taking in the sights. On the contrary, I didn't feel so well while flying on the plane.

As I sat in my seat looking out of the window and around the plane, I slowly felt the gassy results of the last few days, as my stomach was churning up and my knotted up bowels were rumbling away. With a scoured face, I tried to contain myself as I looked across at the two officers to my right with a sourly and churning stomach, but I could not contain nature any longer and let rip with the loudest, smelliest, fart. The results even made my stomach churn as the two officers glared at me unable to move from their seats. If looks could kill those officers would have saved Saddam the job there and then.

Seemingly, the flight dragged on endless for six hours in all, as we passed over Egypt and the Red Sea. And, this was another remarkable

On the plane ready to go.

moment as everyone scrambled quick for their cameras ensued, such as Japanese tourists in the middle of London for the day. As the sun was setting we knew it wouldn't be much longer for our Tri-Star landed at its destination.

The aircraft landed safely in Saudi Arabia at 5:30p.m. The plane's doors opened monotonously, letting the desert air burst in spryly, deathly hot, arid and sticky. It was dark when we walked down the steps of the aircraft and onto the runway, where Bell AH-1 Cobra gun ships lined the sides of the runway and made this airport not just the same as any other airport. From the plane, we got off, and we marched straight over and boarded two coaches to take us to Al Jubayl, a port city on the Persian Gulf similar to my home city of Liverpool, which had evolved around its maritime industry. The journey from the Saudi airport to Al Jubayl took approximately a half hour. The camp was well lit with a high security fence guarded by British and American Contingency force MPs. Once the driver's ID had been checked by the MPs, we were allowed to pass through the gates.

As we drove on, we saw ahead and nearby in the distance what our immediate home looked like. It was a large warehouse, where our kit had been previously dropped off that we had not seen since we were in Soest.

It appeared that I would not only share my new living space with my companions, but, also, with some British Army Air Corps Gazelle helicopters and Bedford trucks, which were stored in this warehouse. We were to book into the warehouse just like booking into the Ritz Hotel, but unfortunately this wasn't the Ritz. When we pulled up to the warehouse, the staff took down our next of kin details, we off-loaded our kit, and, then, we were given something to eat and drink in the form of an army pack lunch, which everyone in the army calls 'death packs' due to its dodgy contents.

As soon as we finished eating and off-loaded our kit, we loaded them onto another coach and moved onto our first military location. And as usual, nobody seemed to know where we were going except for the coach driver. In the darkness of the night, we eventually arrived at our transit accommodation, Archirode camp. Our squadron OC gave us a quick debriefing on the do's and don'ts in the camp, and, once again, we unloaded our kit from the Bedford's. Finally, a Sergeant from the Artillery, who was in charge of the camp, showed us to our billets, which would be our home until our vehicles arrived from Bremerhaven, Germany, by ship.

Some members of Trunk Node 053 in Archiroden camp.

10

The billet, where I stayed, was small and equipped with only two rooms, bunk beds down each side for twenty blokes; however, we did have our own en suite toilet and shower. When I got settled, I stowed my kit and eventually wrote Paula the first of many bluey's. Once everyone had written their bluey's home, and before I retired for the evening, I gathered all the bluey's together, walked out of the billet and took them round to the post box. The post box was made from a cardboard box and was situated at the camp's guardroom right at the front gates.

I woke up early in the morning in an unfamiliar surrounding, seeing the sun shine and glare through the window, closing my eye lids from the brightness of the sunlight. I knew by the weight of my eyes that I hadn't had much sleep. The camp resembled the set of *Carry on up the Khyber*, a film I saw as a young boy, barrack blocks and sand - lots of sand, and the only people who seemed to be working were the troggies (*name given to describe a local native*). The Arabs dressed in woolly jumpers and balaclavas. Everywhere I looked the troggies worked quite happily in jumpers and jeans, as we merely sweltered away in thin T-shirts and shorts during the Arab nation's winter. Nevertheless, their winter weather was extremely hot to us with the heat being in the region of 70 degrees Fahrenheit and blistering down upon us.

The familiar chubby figure of Staff Large entered our billets with the best of news of the day, which was we had a NBC lesson. The NBC lessons were vital to our survival if Saddam decided to use such biological and/or chemical weapons on us as he had done in the past in the Iran-Iraq war of the 1980's. The NBC suit was the most uncomfortable piece of equipment the Army ever gave me to wear. The suit was the MK-IV DPM (*disruptive pattern material*) version and heavily lined with charcoal and for obvious reasons not exactly made of breathable materials. The extremely heavy suit, along with a cumbersome S10 respirator made our lessons seem twice as long and twice as hard as they ever were before. Staff Large forcibly ran us ragged for our own good when we carried out the inarguable and torturous drills in the overwhelming heat of the desert, as he repeatedly said, "This is for your own good!"

The afternoon was incredibly hot, and we got some of our own free time to do as we pleased, for Saddam, in addition, and more importantly, our military machine weren't quite ready to fight yet. As a result of this, we left the camp for Pearl Beach, which was the HQ of 4 Brigade and a short walk from our camp. That day, I lay quietly on the hot sandy beach catching some UV's (*ultra violet rays*) from the sun. While I lay on the sand, I looked at a crystal clear aqua-blue sea, along with the overcast cloudy sky above, thinking that I could stay here during the war. Surprisingly, I met up with some of my old mates that day, Arnie, Hobbsie, and Selly, amongst others from my parent unit 3 Div who'd also been deployed with 4 Brigade. Anyway, my own relaxing time of relish came to an abrupt stop because we had to pack up and be back at the camp promptly at 4:00 p.m. We arrived back in time for tea, and we got a Sunday roast. After tea, I spent the rest of the evening listening to music cassettes on my personnel stereo and writing blueys to the lads back home although I didn't have much to tell them because I had only been at the camp for one day.

The next morning we were awoken early for PT (*physical training*) and the sun was already up, shinning brightly and the heat from it was beating down upon us. The run we had was shorter than usual, in comparison to the hard long runs in Germany because nobody could hold any sort of pace for too long, not even the wiry PTI's (*physical training instructors*). The day continued with weapon training, sucking eggs, going over the rudiments of our personnel-weapon the SLR, along with how many rounds we should put into the magazine because we were in sandy conditions and would only be putting in fifteen rounds into the magazine, instead of the maximum twenty rounds. This was to prevent the rounds from jamming and how to keep it free from sand and in working order as if we had never been taught. Later, as the day progressed, I found out that I was on every soldier's pet hate, stag (*guard duty*). And, the biggest bummer was that night was Christmas Eve. Everyone hated staging on over the Christmas period.

The stag wasn't so bad, indeed, with two hours on and four hours off, I was able to live with that because the weather was good, and I had plenty of time to write bluey's home to Paula, for I really missed her. I finished my stag, and realised it was Christmas Day. Because I was up all night, a swampy vague smell omitted from me, and I knew a shower was in order. As I arrived at the billet, the others were leaving for the church parade; as a result of being on stag all night long, I didn't even want to go to the parade, and I didn't.

'CHRISTMAS DAY 1990'

Staff Large arrived like some camouflaged Father Christmas with a postal sack full of parcels for everyone in the billet from the Royal British Legion. My parcel contained soaps, sweets, a torch and a letter from the legion reminding me that those at home had not forgotten about us out here in the Gulf. That Christmas Day everyone was lucky because nobody needed to be on duty, and we all headed off down to the beach, had some fun and relaxed from our normal duties.

I never dreamt that I would be spending Christmas Day on a beach soaking up the UV's. In a sad but enrapturing sort of way, I laid on the soft sandy beach with my eyes closed thinking about what I'd be doing if I were back at home in Liverpool with my friends and family. Usually, I'd be drinking down in the local pub, the 'Highwayman' on Belle Vale estate with my dad, and then, we'd go home for dinner, and after dinner - the Queen's eminent speech. And, then, I'd have some more beer and off to bed for a short hour or two nap before going out for the evening. Nevertheless, reality hit me when I opened my eyes and saw the beauty of the copasetic surroundings of the sandy beach, the palm trees and other brush as well as the clear blue water. I just kept my mind on next year's Christmas. But this year, my Christmas dinner consisted of Camel burger and chips: not that they where made of camels.

I chatted to some of the lads from 4 Brigade. I turned to my fellow sun worshiper, Jay, and said in a lighten voice, "Can you imagine all of our families back home if they could see us now."

Sarcastically, he replied, "Yeah, I bet they think we are having a really hard time in the trench's," Jay replied, and we laughed.

The photographer from *Soldier Magazine* appeared and interrupted our sun bathing and lavish Christmas dinner. Eventually, we formed up as soldierly as we could into something resembling a military unit; in addition, some of the boys maintained the festive spirit by wearing Father Christmas hats. Remarkably, this was an opportunity for the squadron's OC to take some snap shots for the corps' magazine called *The Wire*.

The snap of that picture ended the day's festivities on the beach before we were ordered to gather our kit and return to camp.

Once again, when we got back home in camp, we dropped our kit at the camp cookhouse and ventured inside, which had been set up in the fullest of military tradition, were all senior ranks, including officers, served the troops with their Christmas dinner. On entering the cookhouse, Staff Large, everybody's favourite Staff Sergeant, singled me out. "Molloy" He said and continued, "How long have you been in the Army?" He said loudly with a sarcastic sneer.

With whimsy witticism I replied, "Long enough Staff."

Staff Larges reaction to my less than courteous reply was to order me to a table raised on a stage at the very front of the cookhouse, where other young soon to be victims waited in anticipation. Once everybody was in place eagerly awaiting the slop jockeys culinary delights, the officers began to wait on our tables baying to our demands. Christmas Day was the only time in the British Army the humble squaddie gets waited on hand and foot by anybody.

The traditions of the junior rank's mess were not to be forgotten just because we were in the middle of some god-forsaken hole. The inevitable began when rock hard roasties (*roast potatoes*) and peas became missiles, and most of them were aimed at the top table, where I was sitting. It then dawned on me why Staff Large wanted me to sit at the raised table on the stage. At that precise moment, one of the lads screamed, "Food fight!"

Those words sent our now unwilling skivvies running for cover in the kitchen. The battle had begun, and I dived for cover under the table clutching a handful of roasties off my plate. The eight bodies that Staff Large singled out crouched beneath our table. Anything or any kind of food we could lay our hands on from peas to paper plates crashed aimlessly across the cookhouse. I had no chance to retaliate on any individual, so I took a blind shot into the middle of the crowd, and boy did I put some force in it. The roastie found its mark on the front of a Sergeant's head and splattered as he ran for cover. I dived back behind the table and tried to avoid getting hit with anything. As soon as I'd gotten down behind the table with smug satisfaction, a barrage of assorted nuts smashed around us like a downpour of hail stones. Major Bell, our squadron OC, abruptly brought the fun and games to an end when he entered the room; moreover, this brought the day's festivities to an end. Major Bell was tall and slender with ginger hair, and we didn't want to remain in his company, so we left the cookhouse in a right state for the hired help to clean up the mess as we all retired to our billets for the evening.

Pearl Beach, Saudi Arabia, Christmas Day 1990.

Back at the billet I sat on my bunk, reflecting back on the day's events as my thoughts turned towards home and Paula. I toiled over the fairly fabulous fun-filled day, home and Paula. And as usual, I grabbed my mail and collected up the lad's mail and took a slow stroll to the post box at the guardroom that night. I took precise pictures of today's beach activities and sent the photographic evidence back home to Paula, so she could develop it for me. On my return to the billet, a few of us lads talked and laughed about the day we had before retiring for the night.

Boxing Day began with me and the rest of the troop doing our dobhi (*laundry*), or a poor attempt at trying to wash, through a pair of combats in a sink the size of a teacup, and, then, rinsing them out as best as I could. The fun was not to end as I had the means to dry the clothes, as did half the billet as we turned the surrounding area into something resembling a Chinese laundry. The heat of the Saudi Arabian winter sun dried our clothes in no time at all. While we grabbed this rare free time to do our dobhi, Lieutenant Naden had left camp to visit RHQ to find out if our vehicles had arrived from Germany and if we had any orders (*military instructions*) to move to a new location.

On returning back to camp, Lieutenant Naden had with him orders from RHQ that our vehicles and equipment had finally been unloaded off the container ships from Germany and were awaiting our arrival at the port for collection. We mounted up on the few Bedford trucks we had and headed off for the port of Al Jubayl.

Me in my 1 Ton Land Rover (Battle Bus) with little Greeny when we went to the port to pick up our vehicles

11

On our way to Al Jubayl, the sun was beating down upon us and the heat was unbearable; thus, the only consolation was the cool breeze off the sea. For the first time, we drove pass a group of allied American troops that were going in the opposite direction. Attentively, one of the boys pointed in their general direction screaming, "Hey look at those Spams."

I naively proclaimed to my neighbour, "What's a Spam?"

With amusement, he told me that the word SPAM stood for 'Spastic Plastic American Mother fuckers.' But, when I asked him where he got the origin of the name from, he didn't know. The name must have come from long ago and stuck with the Brit's. Sweat dripped from us, and we all just wanted to get to where we were going. It was not too long before we arrived at the port Al Jubayl and found our vehicles parked nose to tail. In true military fashion, the order of the day was to hurry up and wait, which was the norm even in wartime; so we found. We just seemed to sit there with nobody quite knowing what was to happen next, so we used this time to take more photographs.

At this point in the campaign, I began to feel down, depressed, and began to talk to a friend, Jay, yet I never did tell him why I was depressed. I picked myself up and went for a walk with my Gat simply because everywhere I went my Gat came with me. Gradually, terribly bad thoughts began to race through my mind, and then, tears began to stream down my cheeks, and after walking a few yards down the rows of parked vehicles, I sluggishly slumped to the ground and hysterically cried out, "Why? Why? Why?"

All I wanted to do was kill myself right there and then to make my heartache go away.

I turned my Gat around and put the muzzle in my mouth, wrapping my lips tightly around it, peering down the long barrel. I moved my hands down the length of the Gat towards the trigger, images of what could have been raced through my mind, and I managed to reach the trigger with my right thumb, but I could not bring myself to apply that final pressure down onto it to end my pain. I pulled the Gat away and regretfully sunk my head between my knees. My mind was about to explode with the thought of the woman I loved taking the life of our unborn child. I got reasserted when Lieutenant Baker explicitly discovered me alone with my Gat and rolling tears drying on my cheeks.

Lieutenant Baker, being one of our better officers, sat with me while I reflectively explained to him about why I was in such a state of depression. Lieutenant Baker sat and listened attentively to my problems in regards to the situation. I explained to him how Paula told me about the abortion on my last leave and how it seemingly didn't affect me and it really didn't sink in before we were deployed to the Gulf. At no point during the conversation did Lieutenant Baker reprimand or judge me in any way; furthermore, the incident of our talk remained between the two of us and was never mentioned nor talked about ever again. Now, my mind was clear and my focus was back to the job at hand. I soldiered on with the feeling that a great weight had been lifted off of my shoulders, for we eventually took possession of our vehicles and made our way back to camp.

On our arrival back at camp, we were informed that a telephone trip had been arranged to take us to Camp 4. Going to Camp 4 lifted my spirits because I would be able to speak to Paula by using our free phone cards, which were donated by the Royal British Legion. Sergeant Clay told me in a sympathetic and orderly way, "Molloy! Make your way to the troop recce Land Rover to meet Staff Large and me or else you will miss your opportunity to call your bird."

Sergeant Clay, a burly bloke, who had a few years left to serve in the army, was our troop's recce Sergeant and I was his driver - Rad Op. Anxiously, Sergeant Clay raced off with all of the lads in our unit in tow back through the town of Al Jubayl on our way to Camp 4. As we expeditiously raced through the streets, the sights resembled the streets of Bradford with all the troggies going about their business. Once we arrived at Camp 4, the queues for the public telephones that had been installed in the camp for the exclusive use for squaddies, tailed back the length of several billets, and the wait was even longer because most of the phones were out of order.

Finally, my turn had come to use the phone, and I was lucky enough to get through the first time I called. Paula had just walked through the door from work. She was shocked to her my voice, for I was the last person she expected to hear from, but, sadly, I didn't have much time to talk; indeed, I only had a few moments, which was just enough time to tell her that I loved her and missed her very much. My few short moments alone with Paula were shattered by the awfully meek tones of Sergeant Clay,

"Come on, Scouse. It's time to go."

I said goodbye to Paula then slowly placed the handset on the receiver whilst reflecting on our short conversation. After composing myself, I jumped into the back of the Land Rover and Sergeant Clay drove us back to camp, so we could settle down for the evening because we would be moving location the following day.

The day drew to a close and the night crept upon me, as I settled down with a bluey and my thoughts to Paula. I wrote to her, letting her know how this would be my last day at camp because we were headed off out into the desert in the morning. I wrote to friends at home informing them of my movements, knowing that they would read each letter. As usual, I gathered up the lad's letters from the billet and took the short trip to the guardroom dropping the letters in the cardboard post box. That was the night everybody wrote home expressively because nobody knew when they would have the chance to write home again.

The journey we were about to take would be a long uneasy trip into the unknown. We left the secure confines of the camp straight after breakfast, and I took my place right next to Sergeant Clay in our recce 1-Tonnie (*1 Ton Land Rover)* that was just behind the troop OC's 110 Land Rover. Our journey north on the motorway took us deep into a virtual lunar landscape of sand as far as the eye could see; also, I spotted the first glimpse of wild camels roaming aimlessly along with calves in tow, which was the first time I saw these ships of the desert but not the last.

On our way into the Saudi Arabian desert.

Always getting bogged in on our way to our first location.

Several signposts had been sprayed over with paint, but I distinctively made out the word Kuwait with an arrow pointing straight up. The sign was printed in English, Arabic and there also was some other indistinct place that nobody cared about. We continued to drive until Sergeant Clay unexpectedly turned of the road right and carried on driving aggressively for another fifteen minutes, and, then, he abruptly turned left onto a sandy track and continued to drive with more quickness, and we managed to stay right on his bumper. From here on in, the desert's sandy and sometimes hobbley track would be the road we followed before we arrived at our pre-planned location.

On the way there, Sergeant Clay somehow managed to bog down our 1-Tonnie in some soft sand. We were stuck out in the desert until two lads came to our assistance in their 1-Ton Land Rover. It was Scouse Robbo and his recce Sergeant, Joe, and they were both from another troop. Scouse Robbo and I wedged the steel sand tracks under the front tyres in the hope that they would free us of the soft sand. We had brought the steel sand tracks with us from Germany for situations just like the one we were in now. Eventually, after hours of cursing and trying to get the 1-Tonnie back onto hard sand, we did manage to free the vehicle from the soft sand while the entire troop drove right passed us and set up camp at our new

Scouse Robbo.

location. Nevertheless, we finally got the Land Rover back on track and made it to our new location.

Nobody seemed to know how long we would spend here in this location out in the hot arid desert of Saudi Arabia. We settled into the location only in a matter of hours and managed to help the slop jockeys erect the cookhouse tent. My personal moral and that of some of my mates had hit rock bottom. We hastily wasted enough time, so I decided to set up my bed for the night in the constricted confines of the back of my 1-Tonnie. The space I had was limited for two reasons; first, my space measured roughly 4ft x 2ft. Secondly, in an instance, Sergeant Clay made himself comfortable inside the majority of a central space of the vehicle with a metal-framed bed and mattress, which he had 'acquired' back in Germany. In the morning after a broken night of sleep, Sergeant Clay informed me that I was to put up my new home in the form of a 9ft x 9ft tent and had to share it with Jim, Lieutenant Naden's driver - Rad Op. I didn't really know Jim Watson that well, but he came from Southern England and was around the same age as myself, 20. Jim and I erected the tent near the front of our location with the rest of Node's vehicles and tents behind us.

12

No sooner had we set up our new home, we had little if any time to lose in regularly preparing our vehicles for the day's normal recce patrol. The OC and Sergeant Clay, got in and headed off in the 110 Land Rover, so Jim and I set off for the day in the 1-Tonnie closely following the OC and Sergeant Clay, who were travelling far ahead of us in the OC'S 110 Land Rover, in order to reconnaissance future locations for our Node. As the day drawn on; the heat kept rising to unbearable hot temperatures. On the long drive in the blazing hot desert to recce a new location for our Node, Jim and I slowly finished talking about football, women and ended on the character assassination talk of our fellow travelers, Sergeant Clay and Lieutenant Naden. Jim asked me, "What do you think of Sergeant Clay?" "Not much. A bit of sly bastard at times." I scrawled my reply.

Jim and I continued talking about Sergeant Clay, and, once we finished talking about Clay, his travelling companion Lieutenant Naden got it in the neck from Jim. Jim was Lieutenant Naden's driver and radio operator, and when I asked Jim his thoughts on out troop OC Jim stayed quiet for a second and answered with a snarl, "I've never really liked him from the first day I met him. He thinks because he's the boss he can do what he wants to people like us."

Jim didn't think much of him, but he wasn't all that bad as bosses go. I had a difference of opinion to Jim with regards to Lieutenant Naden because I had managed to have a pint and a chat with him on our ferry from Calais to Dover when the regiment was given five days leave prior to deploying on Op Granby. We even got to talk about our fellow allies, the Americans. However, we hadn't had any contact with the Americans as of yet, but we knew of higher-ranking officers who had been in contact with the Americans.

Driving along a seemingly endless dirt road following behind the OC's 110 Land Rover, a camp appeared out of nowhere and as we drove by the camp we saw it was very well camouflaged with camouflage nettings. We pulled up in front of the barrier at the entrance to the camp, where two SPAMs stood on guard. Lieutenant Naden left his vehicle and approached the guards. Jim and I could not hear what was being discussed, but after a few minutes, Lieutenant Naden climbed back into his Land Rover and we sped off leaving the SPAMs coughing in a cloud of dust. That was the first contact Jim and I had with our American cousins, even though we didn't speak to them, just waved hello while we passed through. Once we passed through the camp and after slagging off our travelling companions for another twenty minutes or so, I got bogged down in the 1-Tonnie. Jim thought decisively and thought that he was the better driver; indeed, he thought he'd be able to get us out of this one. Therefore, I humbly climbed down from the driver's seat and let him get on with it, although Sergeant Clay came back in the OC's Land Rover and connected to both vehicles the tow chains that was in the back of his Land Rover and pulled us forward, free from the soft sand and onto harder sand, but Jim never hit the brakes sharp enough, and he smashed right into the rear lights of the OC's Land Rover. Sergeant Clay jumped out screaming, "What the fuck happened, dickhead?"

I smugly stood by, grinning to myself and laughing inside, leaving the Lieutenant Naden bewildered and confused with head in hands because Jim had been behind the wheel. The night was slowly drawing in on us, and we were making our way back to our location when I glanced downward and noticed the fuel indicator was on red. Earlier in the day, we used up our reserve forty litre petrol in the two jerry cans that was always carried on the roof of the 1-Tonnie. I tried frantically to signal Sergeant Clay with my main beam headlights as he drove further on ahead of us, but to no avail they drove away into the distance night not to gander at all behind them.

"Surely, they must have seen the light flashing in the mirrors." Jim exclaimed as panic arose in his voice.

"Well, it's too late now, la. We're all out of petrol," I told Jim.

With my hat in one hand and holding my head with my other hand, Jim and I just sat and watched the OC's Land Rover disappear into the deepest darkened night, watching the Land Rover get smaller and smaller as it moved further away from us. Jim slammed his fist solid onto the dashboard in desperation yelling, "This was no training area in Germany."

Distraught, I replied, "Know, la. This is the real thing. We're nearly at war!"

For what seemed ages, in all of but five minutes, a light appeared in my left wing mirror. As the vehicle drew nearer, the lumbering shape of a Bedford 4-ton truck grew larger and larger until he pulled up just ahead of us. To our great relief, the Bedford was full of jerry cans. Our luck

Trunk Node 053 in the first location.

definitely changed and was with us as it belonged to our squadron and was a POL (*petrol oil and lubricants*) truck. We were only too glad to see our saviour, and we relieved him of two jerry cans of petrol in exchange of my two empty jerry cans, in order to get safely back to our location. Once we had refueled, a set of headlights appeared up ahead, and, eventually, Sergeant Clay emerged from the Land Rover with jerry cans in hand. They never even realized we were not behind them until they arrived back at our location.

When we got back to our location, I was made up just to see my doss bag laid out on the stretcher. I had liberated the stretcher from the Bedford, which was our stores wagon. After all the horror stories I heard about snakes and other nasty creatures that shared the desert with us, the stretcher was a good acquisition. Once again, Lieutenant Naden and Sergeant Clay were successfully ripped by Jim and me to bits after the last fiasco of us running out of petrol and leaving us behind. It wasn't our fault that we ran out of petrol, and because I was really tired, I wasn't going to be bothered arguing with the Lieutenant Naden and Sergeant Clay. Hence, that night I slept well once I had forgotten about the crawlies.

After breakfast word spread around that Major Bell would be visiting all the squadron Nodes in turn. The order went around that we were to

Gas, Gas, Gas!

wear our NBC suits, which would cripple even the fittest man in the stifling heat of the desert, but that suit was a necessity to our survival under the wartime circumstances. The day drew on with the sun at its peak, when, suddenly, Major Bell screamed out warningly at the top off his voice, "Gas! Gas! Gas!"

That was the signal for us to carry out our IA (*immediate action*) drills. All of us in the entire camp, turned our backs to the wind, took deep breaths while we held our eyes tightly shut and reached for our respirators, pulling the straps apart to put them on. Then, I dropped my chin, forced my face into the respirator, pulled the straps as tight as I could around my head and blew out a long breath of air screaming aloud, "Gas! Gas! Gas!"

But, the words were slightly muffled in the confines of my respirator. I found the closest person to me, who was Daz Kirby, as did everybody else, and we buddied up in order to check that our respirators, hoods and gloves were correctly fitted. The whole location remained at full alert while we dug trenches according to the state of alert we were in. The heat from my face fogged up my respirator lenses and sweat from my brow stung my eyes increasing my discomfort and labouring my breath. After this little exercise, we turned the trench into a shallow grave, planting a make shift gravestone made from cardboard and inscribed '14628718 Sig Morale,' for this was a clear opportunity for a photo of us all and our

Digging a stage 3 trench in NBC kit in our first location, December 1990.

After digging the trench in NBC kit in very hot conditions our morale had died, so we buried it!

first causality Sig Morale! I heard one of the lad's mutter, "I am going to shoot that cunt if he tries that trick again."

He was talking about Major Bell making us wear our full NBC kit and digging trenches in the overwhelming desert heat. Everybody seemed exhausted from the heat. Eventually, after spending hours in my full NBC kit and feeling grimy, sweaty and dirty, I went off alone to wash down my bollocks with warm water and a block of soap in hand. I pulled down my combats and boxer shorts to my knees, gripped my soap and sponge in either hand, and I got underway with what seemed a wash of a lifetime. Jay Curly, a so-called mate, decided to take a photo of me in mid flow, laughed, and, then, he said, "There's one for the Corps Magazine, Scouse."

And to our dismay, it was a shame the photo never made it into the magazine.

After a long day of working in those hot NBC suits, I settled down in the admin (*administration*) tent to write Paula another bluey. I wondered what she would be doing tonight with it being New Years Eve. With my eyes closed tight, I tried to imagine what she would look like, and all that I could imagine was her long brown curly hair, green eyes and olive complexion. A sombre mood fell over the tent as most of us gathered our feelings and thoughts and put them onto paper. The tent was partly full with other lads writing bluey's home too. I posted my bluey in our now morale saving cardboard post box, and then, I wondered over to Andy's vehicle to play computer games on his PC (*personal computer*).

There we were, brew on, toast in hand, on the brink of certain war, and we were playing kid's computer games. Still, I couldn't get to grips with all the normal things we were doing taking into consideration of where we were and what we were about to try and accomplish.

Phil in our second location, which was the stone quarry.

13

Lieutenant Naden woke Jim and me up abruptly at 1 o'clock in the morning,

"Come on. Get up! We're moving location now, and I want my Rover ready to move A.S.A.P."

This was a task never done lightly in the Army.

"Okay sir," Jim replied whilst rubbing his eyes and waking up in disbelief.

We rushed around in the dark, packed away our personal kit and pulled down the 9ft x 9ft tent with the full moon's light helping us on in our efforts. The whole Node managed to pack up and was made ready to move in less than an hour and a half, and all fifteen vehicles were made ready to move in the dark. The Node formed up in a tight packet end to end on the track awaiting the order to move when that old army adage sprung to mind again, 'Hurry up and wait,' which we did until the following morning.

The mood amongst us changed considerably from one of tense anticipation to mutterings of rebellion and Major Bell getting it again. We were all terribly pissed off at the Squadron OC, and at this point he was higher up on our hit list than Saddam Hussein. Our SSM (*Squadron Sergeant Major*), WO II O'Reilly, was a short and a slightly over weight Northern Irishman with graying black hair and moustache. He was known as 'PTD - Paddy the dick' amongst the members of our squadron. PTD gathered everybody together from the different Nodes and once again took the opportunity to take yet another photo. Major Bell positioned himself on top of a Bedford proclaiming, "Right, gents look in and smile."

"If anybody here smiles or even looks at the camera they will get five extra duties," said Staff Large."

Since we were not that far into the campaign, even the senior ranks began to crack under the relentless bullshit. As soon as the photo shoot was over, we all disappeared and headed back to our vehicles and their relative shade from the sun.

It appeared as if our move had been delayed, so Staff Large told one of our slop jockeys to unpack some of the kitchen equipment and erect a tent. Now, with there being no set time for us to move location, it was thought best to eat as we didn't know when the chance would arise again for our next meal. After our meal, there was still no news on when we would move out. With it being middle of the day, some of the lads got the volleyball net out and made a court while the rest of us took this lull time to top up our suntans. In my case, I turned more scarlet because of my fair complexion. As the day drew on, moving out was becoming more apparent that we would be remaining here at least another night.

The sun roasted down upon us early the next morning, and I was woken by Sergeant Clay with a tap on my 1-Tonnie's window at six-forty-five in the morning. And, I was told to prepare to move as we had now been given the go ahead for our Node to make its way to the next location. The journey took us about an hour as we traveled in convoy adhering to the British Army's manual of driving. When we arrived at the new location, I thought it wasn't too bad considering where we were, for everywhere we went in the desert had its similarities. This location was a stone-crushing quarry, but it was still in full operational use. Sergeant Clay sent Rick to ask one of the troggies if they would help us settle in by the use of one of their mechanical diggers. The troggy came over in his mechanical digger and Sergeant Clay explained to the driver with sign language that he wanted him to scrape away at the pile of stones, allotting the Relay Bedford's to reverse into the dug out spot. Spread all around us were piles of largely crushed stones. I thought the stones would come in use as cover from any artillery or air bombardment. It took the whole Node a few hours to set up our new home for the foreseeable future. This involved moving vehicles into position and camouflaging them, mainly from enemy aircraft, and, gradually, our new location was being erected, but it wasn't quite finished yet, and I could have really done with it to be erected, for I was in desperate need of a toilet.

Since there wasn't a toilet of ours to use because our camp was just getting erected, I had no alternative except to ask one of the troggies in the site office if I could use their toilet. He pointed his finger in the direction for me to go, and I quickly walked that way, went into the toilet and stood still looking in amazement at what was there instead of a toilet pan. To my awed imagination, there was what I had described to be a porcelain shower tray with foot grips on both sides and coming out of the wall a shower like hose minus the shower head, which I figured was to wash your arse once you've done the business. The way in which I needed to use this so-called toilet dawned on me, and, in desperation, I pulled down my combats and boxer shorts to my ankles and adopted the position on the tray, squatting over the small waste hole. Once I was done with my business, I used the hose to clean myself as there was no toilet paper. This was the first time I had ever used a toilet like this before, and, no doubt, it would not be the last.

And when our location had finally gotten erected, I took a drive to the entrance of the quarry, where I had noticed a troggy shop on my way in. The troggy shop stood alone was a very small building and made up of concrete. This shop sold only a few select items from sweets to cans of lemonade. So, I bought a few cans of lemonade and some bars of chocolate to take back to my new location with me. We either used American dollars or Saudi riyals to buy whatever we wanted.

When I returned to our new location, Jay, Connor and I were detailed by Staff Large to construct a roof out of our camouflage nets for the Rover Park. It was way too hot to do any work; nevertheless, Jay and I enjoyed the weather and had a few laughs as we sewed the nets together. Connor was a miserable bastard, who I don't think I'd seen smile yet. He was a Corporal and a technician, so that explained everything because in the Royal Signals many of the technicians are renowned for being all work and no play, with their supposedly superior intelligence. On the other side, once the Relay lads got their comms shots in with other nodes, we stood down for the evening except for me, because Staff Large solely ordered me to go and stag on at the entrance of our location until they could get someone to relieve me. I got used to staging on because I knew there was a lot of it to come. I wondered if Staff Large would ever put his name and the rest of the senior ranking NCO's names on the stag list, for some reason I don't think so. I understood that in peace time the senior ranks and officers would not do any stags, but we were not in peace time we were in war time, and we were in a situation were everyone needed to do their bit to watch each other's back. I thought I would be staging on for awhile, but, suddenly, I was relieved after two hours were I made good my escape from my post, and, then, I got on and put up my tent with Jim.

It was New Years Day, and that signalled the day our 6-month tour of duty officially started, and I didn't know what was installed for me. It was a lot easier this time to put the tent up with it being daylight. Jay had nowhere to sleep, so we told him that he could sleep in our tent. At the time, I didn't know how much Jay would end up becoming a real good mate or not because I had only talked to him on a couple of occasions back in Germany. With Jay becoming our new flat mate, space would become very limited inside the tent. Jay and Jim made their beds along the sides of the tent, and I slept crossways on my bed at the back of the tent. It was very cramped indeed, and I now knew what it is like for an Asian family to live in a council flat in Bradford because they had generations of families living in the one flat.

In the morning the tent stunk awfully of body odour, and it took some getting used to. After breakfast, we were all split up into work parties, digging three trenches, one by the Relay wagons, one by Node Command and the other at the front of our location. I was helping to dig the trench by Node command. These were used for staging on. With a slight breeze in the air, the sand was swirling all around us making it difficult to see and difficult to dig. All the digging was thirsty work, and we all went through about five litres of water in two hours. We were near completion of the trench and the filling of sandbags when it began to rain. After we dug and filled sand bags for five hours, I began to pray for some kind of relief, and I felt as if God had answered my prayers. I felt each individual cool wet raindrop as they splashed down on my face and the rest of my body. In comparison, it was the best feeling I felt since Everton Football Club won the European Cup Winners Cup in 1985. It only rained for a couple of hours, and then, Staff Large came over with more green sandbags to be filled. The filled sandbags were used to build walls for the trenches. By building up around the sides of the trenches, it meant less digging down. I soon realized that there wouldn't be enough sandbags for the job. I noticed Rick down in the heart of our location heading towards the admin tent.

"Rick, Rick, Rick" I shouted at the top of my voice and continued, "Do us a favour? Ask the Q if he's got any more sand bags."

Rick looked over at me and gave me a thumbs up, to signal he had heard me. About five minutes later Rick shouted at me, "Scouse! The Q said he hasn't got any more left until the next boat comes in."

Consequently, we were unable to continue filling more sandbags, and the trenches were left nearly half-completed, and nobody knew when the boat was going to arrive with fresh supplies.

14

As I entered the main admin tent, where we had our meals, one of the lads had the blue mail sack on the table sorting out today's mail. At this time of day, when the mail arrived, the admin tent got really busy with lads desperate to hear from back home. Gaz Tuff, one of the Relay Corporals, called out people's names as he distributed the mail, and excitement radiated and showed on their faces when their names were shouted out as they collected their mail. On some other lad's faces, the excitement was eradicated when they received no mail.

"Scouse," Gaz screamed my name across the tent.

"Yeah," I replied eagerly with a broad beaming smile on my face and my hopes raised thinking that I'd received a letter from Paula.

"No mail." Gaz teasingly screamed back at me.

And, the tent erupted with fits of laughter.

"You fucking twat!" I screamed back with disgust because my hopes had gotten arose.

Then, I fell back down gradually but with a big bang. This practice of getting the lads hopes up with the mail dates back to long before I joined the army and will no doubt continue long after I leave the army because the lads get a good laugh out of it. I was able to laugh the joke off, as I knew it would be something I would do too. We shouldn't really joke about the mail because the mail was taken quite seriously. It was such a morale booster when a person received mail. Numerous overwhelming dull faces, including mine, had left the tent when the mail sack got held upside down and no more mail came out. So, I went back into my tent to try and forget about today's mail drop, knowing there was always tomorrow's mail drop. I slumped down on my doss bag with my head back and eyes wide open looking at the roof the tent while feeling pissed off that I hadn't received any mail yet. My tent was erected adjacent to the admin tent and I could hear the muffled voice of Sergeant Clay inside the admin tent asking the lads if any of them knew where I was, but I couldn't be bothered with leaving the tranquillity of my tent.

Sergeant Clay tracked me down, along with the other lads to go back to our previous location to pick up the field toilet cubicles. When we reached our previous location the field toilet cubicles stood out as they were the only man made object in the open desert. The field toilets had been constructed out of soft wood timber by the Royal Engineers in Al Jubayl and there were three toilet cubicles to the one set of field toilets. Cut down oil drums with a blue liquid chemical inside to prevent disease collected the human excrement and urine. Once the oil drums were full, they would be dragged out by who ever was on shit burning duty and they would pour petrol and diesel into the oil drum and set the contents on fire. This was to ensure the risk of disease was kept to a minimum. Once the fire had gone out, the left over contents of the oil drum was buried in a pit. It took all of us to man handle the field toilets onto the back of the POL wagon and once it was secured we made our way back to our new location.

On our return, the field toilets were unloaded on a hill by the plateau and given to the Relay lads for them to convert into showers. The Relays never do much of anything when they're off shift, and for that purpose, they were in charge of the task of converting the toilets into showers. The Relays have a three man det (*detachment*) and each man would work an eight hour shift with sixteen hours off. During their time on shift they had to maintain the comms shots didn't drop, which wasn't very demanding, so they mostly sat in the back of their wagons and played on their PCs, read novels or drank brews. I chuckled at the thought of people back home worrying themselves over us out here in the desert. But, if only the people back home knew what really went on in the back of a Relay wagon then there would be no need to worry because the Relays didn't do any hard or dangerous work.

The two people who worked the hardest out here in the desert were our Army Catering Corps slop jockeys, Hutch and Tosh. Hutch was a Corporal and Tosh was a Private, and both of them had to prepare meals three times a day for forty-two men. I didn't know how they coped in this heat because it was roasting in the cook tent. The food is a mixture of fresh and compo rations. Compo rations were the army's pre-packed tined and packet food. It was the job of our Q to return to Al-Jubayl each day for the re-supply of our rations as well as our mail. We didn't know how long the supply of fresh rations would last, but it was good while we were getting them. Hutch could knock up a gourmet meal out of a ten-man ration pack fit enough for the Queen to eat. For breakfast we had the usual fry up, including a choice of three cereals. For dinner it was always a choice of a wide selection of sandwiches. But, indeed, the best mealtime of the day was tea. We were spoilt for choice with three main courses and three desserts. The food was of a very high standard all the time and we all had Hutch and Tosh to thank for that and for not making the lads go hungry.

After tea, the Q came around and told us to gather at the back of his wagon to be issued with our desert combat uniform. Everyone was excited with this news, it was a new little morale booster for us all. At long last, we would no longer look out of place in the desert with our temperate uniforms, which were more suitable for the green fields and forests of Northern Europe rather than the open deserts of Saudi Arabia. We were issued with 1 x Desert floppy hat, 1 x Sunglasses, 1 x Ski goggles, 1 x Desert combat trousers, 1 x Desert combat jacket and 2 x Sweat rags. All of the senior ranks were issued with desert DPM helmet covers, and all the junior ranks were well pissed off because they didn't get issued with the desert DPM helmet covers. The senior ranks were jack bastards who were only out for themselves, and their attitudes grew irksome and worse and more of us junior ranks got pissed off with the senior ranks. A rift started between the junior and senior ranks; it irritably got wider as each day had gone by. My own patience started to run thin with Sergeant Clay. He let anybody use my 1-Tonnie without informing me as of who was taking it. I knew he was the Sergeant, and I was only a lowly Signalman, however, I was responsible for that vehicle from keeping it clean to the maintenance. We needed to maintain our equipment so that it operated flawlessly, and, therefore, we operated effectively when the time came for war. Every time I got the Rover back, it was full of rubbish like empty crisp packets and empty Pepsi Cola cans, and nobody ever filled it up with petrol on their return.

We'd been in Saudi Arabia a fortnight now, time was flying by quickly and the worse thing for me at that particular moment was that I had no mail coming in from back home. Apart from that and the senior ranks, I really enjoyed it over here. Sometimes, I didn't even bother going in the admin tent for mail call, for I'd only come out on a real downer when my name wasn't shouted out. It was not worth the heartache. I kept praying that I'd get a bluey soon because I wrote home to Paula every night and tonight would be no different. Once I posted my bluey to Paula in the cardboard box, I decided to have an early night because I would be working on the POL wagon park the following day.

It was an incredibly hot day, the Relay lads started to work on the conversion of the field toilets to showers while I helped Staff Large fix the roof on the POL wagon park that was made from camouflage nets. The day was so hot that it was almost too much to bear. So, I took my T-shirt off to catch some UV's. I wasn't going to come all this way without going back without a bronzy. I started to catch the sun, and I felt it as it burnt my back. I should have put my factor twenty sun block on this morning in order to stop me from turning into a lobster. Flinnie and Jay came over to where we were working and told Staff Large that they were going to Flinnie's parent's house in Riyadh to pick up a freezer for the slop jockeys. Both of Flinnie's parents were working in Saudi Arabia and had lived there for some time. This wasn't the first time Flinnie had taken someone to his parent's home while he's been here. He took a few of the lad's back to his parent's house on Christmas Day for their dinner. They all got pissed while they were there, lucky bastards.

I can vividly remember that specific day because I was still on guard duty in the morning when Flinnie came up to the camp gates just hanging around. A Captain from the Artillery, who couldn't mind his own business, shouted over to Flinnie and asked him why he was loitering by the camp gates. The Captain didn't know what to do or say when Flinnie informed him he was waiting to be picked up by his mam and dad. The Captain stood there bewildered, for he wasn't quite expecting that answer. Once it had sunk in, the Captain turned around in the opposite direction and went about his business, which made Flinnie and I laugh to one another.

After our tea that evening, I took the short ten minute drive to a different troggy shop down the road, which was also a garage on the junction of the MSR (*main supply route*). This MSR was codenamed 'Dodge'. I was going to buy some bars of chocolate and cans of lemonade. Inside the shop was a SPAM having a look around. He spotted me and came over to chat. He asked me about my Gat with obvious interest. I gave him a full description of my SLR. He was surprised when I told him that the calibre was 7.62mm.

"God damn. That's an elephant gun," he shrieked excitedly in his southern American accent.

Also, I informed him that it weighed over nine pounds with an empty magazine and over eleven pounds with a full magazine of twenty rounds.

"We only load the magazine with fifteen rounds in desert conditions," I also informed him expertly.

His M16 Automatic Assault Rifle was no match for my SLR. The M16 was lightweight and made mostly of plastic, and it felt more like a toy gun. I finished my friendly chat with the SPAM and headed back to my location with supplies of chocolate and drinks.

Me at the desert barbers.

15

As I returned back to my location, I noticed Jim was staging on at the entrance. I pulled up next to him to take the piss, when, with a gleaming smile on his face, he said, "There's a letter for you on the table in the admin tent, and I think it's from your bird."

That was music to my ears and put a broad smile on my face as my heart started to pound rapidly. Instantaneously, I sped away from Jim with my tyres screeching and leaving Jim in a blinding cloud of dust. I parked the 1-Tonnie up in the Rover Park, gathered up my shopping and nimbly sprinted to the admin tent. The tent was empty, although I could see a pink envelope on the table that sat all alone. As I made my way closer to the table, I made out the name and address written on the envelope, and it read:

24792418 Sig Molloy

TN 053

3 Sqn.

1 A.D.S.R.

B.F.P.O. 649

"Yes!" I screamed out in enjoyment because the letter was from Paula. I was able to tell by her handwriting, which leant slightly to the right. When I picked the letter up off of the table with my right hand, I could smell perfume, and it was Calvin Klein's Obsession, which was Paula's favourite fragrance. The pungent smell of that perfume brought flooding back all the memories as a small lump grew up in my throat. With excitement, I tore the envelope in half; undoubtedly, the letter was still in tact. I looked for the date first and saw that the letter was written on 17/12/90. The letter was certainly a long one.

Paula wrote, "I cried my eyes out on the platform of Lime Street train station, has I waved your train good bye on your return to Germany." And, she continued, "I love you so much, and I want you home, now."

Paula had been referring to the five days leave that the regiment had been given the previous month before we left Germany to deploy on Operation Granby. A tear flowed out of my eye and trickled down my left cheek and nose has I placed the letter in my back pocket. I was happy now that I had received my first letter from Paula. Finally, I stopped worrying.

The next day after breakfast, Rick and I took the wastewater and rubbish down to the tip in a 110 Land Rover, which was half way between our location and the troggy shop on the MSR. When we pulled up, we noticed a couple of SPAMs burning their rubbish. It was very important that the rubbish was burnt to prevent the outbreak of any diseases. They must've been using the same tip as us, so we got out of our Land Rover and started to talk to them. One of them said he was from Texas, and that he was in Panama before he came over here. He bragged about it like the Yanks in general do brag about things. I played the situation as if I was the gullible limey, when really I thought he was a right tosser. I gave Rick a hand to unhitch the trailer, so we could put our waste on the burning embers, and it didn't take long for our rubbish to burn. Once we made sure all of our waste kindled and had been cremated to total ash, we made our way back to our location still taking the piss out of the SPAMs as we drove.

There wasn't much happening for the rest of that day. So, I took this opportunity to give my Gat and magazines a good clean. It was very important that we kept on top of our weapon cleaning because we may need that weapon one day to save our lives. I couldn't imagine anything worse than getting caught in a fire fight and not being able to return fire because my weapon jammed. For that main reason, I treated my weapon with respect. I know it seems pointless to clean anything in the desert because of the sand and dust, but I still made sure to keep on top of it. Once this tedious task was over, I wrote some more blueys to send back home and let them know how things were over here. And, I just hoped to receive another letter from home to boost my morale. When the mail came round today, I received a letter from my insurance company informing me that they had started debiting my account of £20 a month for my insurance endowment policy. When we were told that we were to come out here in the desert, there was a big flap on in our barracks in Germany for everyone to take out some form of life insurance on themselves, so that they were well covered just in case someone came back in a body bag.

Meanwhile, the Q brought a television and video into the admin tent for everyone to use when we had some spare time. I set up the tele and video and put on the 'Soul to Soul' music video in which we received from the Royal British Legion for Christmas. The amount of times the tape got rewound and played again and again during tea was unbelievable as this

Clarky 'Staging on'.

was the first time we had watched the tele for a while. After tea, Staff Large ordered the whole node on parade. He tried to give us a bollocking, but he couldn't do it to save his life, and I understood where he was coming from because whoever was last up in the admin tent last night left it in a right shit tip.

"If anything like this happens again, with leaving the fucking tent in shit state, I'll lock away the tele and video. You've been warned!" He screamed in an orderly and angrily voice.

When he dismissed us, everyone was slagging him off over his voice. Then, out of nowhere, a couple SPAM trucks, which were filled with SPAMs, came into our location. The SPAMs gave us loads of slabs of Pepsi Cola and Sprite Lemonade. They also gave Staff Large a load of cam net poles for our cam nets. We had brought with us old tree branches from Germany to keep our cam nets up, but the branches weren't that sturdy. Hence, the cam net poles from the SPAMs worked much better.

Our Ministry of Defence didn't issue its forces with any decent kit like the SPAMs got issued from their military. Whether our top brass thought that we should suffer or our glorious politicians, who always sung our praises, wouldn't release the cash to make the life of a humble squaddie more bearable, I never knew. The problem with the SPAMs was that they got all the quality top notch military kit like state of the art personal weapons and anti-tank attack helicopters, but they didn't know how to use it and we Brits, the best army in the world, hadn't got that quality top notch military kit, but we knew how to use it. If only our politicians spent money on our forces and provided them with decent kit, no one would dare mess with the Brits. The one very noticeable thing that seemed strange to us Brits and stood out quite trifle was the fact that there were women in their ranks. There were two particular women who were blonde and very nice looking. Not being used to women within our troops, a gang of our lads swarmed all around the two fit blond haired women.

One of their blokes came over to me and introduced himself. He sat down opposite me and we began to chat. He was a reserve soldier and was called up to duty when Iraq invaded Kuwait in August. The conversation led up to our families and the other normal things we talked about when we met someone for the fist time. He reached inside the pocket of his coat and pulled out his wallet. Then, out of his wallet, he pulled out a photograph of a woman. "This is my wife," he said, sporting a wide grin.

She looked Spanish, as did he.

"Very nice," I replied while nodding my head at the same time.

All the while, I thought to myself that she wasn't really that nice looking at all, in fact, she was ugly as sin, but I couldn't actually say that she was a pig to his face. She would have looked good on our pig board amongst the loads of photos of ugly women already pinned on it, which was hanging up in the admin tent. We all wrote to women, known as 'pen pigs,' and if they sent us photos, we picked out the ugly ones and pinned them up. After all the pleasantries were over with the SPAM I'd just met, I got down to business. "Have yeah got any kit you want to swap," I asked him?

"I've got a few things you might be interested in," he replied.

So, I pulled out my beret because all the SPAMs went mad for these berets back in Al Jubayl. The reason that they went so mad for the berets was that only the American Special Forces got to wear berets. "I'll trade yeah me beret for a set of yeah desie combats?" I asked him.

All of us Brits were after a set of SPAM desert combats because we thought theirs were better than ours, and it was pretty common to see British soldiers mixing other army's uniforms, along with their own issued uniforms.

"Gee, that'll be swell, but I ain't got my desert combats yet," he answered in disappointment.

Nevertheless, it was worth a try on my part. The SPAMs stayed for about an hour before they had to get back to their own location. Therefore, we all shook hands and wished each other good night and good luck.

The following day, the Q finally received more sandbags, so we spent the rest of the day finishing off building the three trenches. That particular day wasn't so bad, for it wasn't as hot or as windy as normal. The day was just bearable. On the other hand, the work we did was just as thirsty and sweaty with the need for loads of breaks. Whilst digging the trench, I thought to myself, "I couldn't be a labourer on a building site. Fuck digging holes for a living."

I managed to get out of the hard work early, so that I could do my dobhi before I had to stag on. This was my first opportunity to get my clothes clean for ages. It's been so long, my socks were starting to walk by themselves.

Once again, it came round for my turn to stag on. The time was an early 10 a.m., and I knew that I'd be there till midday. There wasn't much happening that day for us, but the troggies were still working the day away. We were able to look out for miles from where our guard post was situated; however, there wasn't too much to see in front of me except for a huge stone crusher, to my right I only saw the desolated desert, to my left were little mounds of stones scattered round and behind me was our location. I spent the stag recording a message to Paula on a personnel cassette player. It was full of sloppy recordings, such as I miss you, and I love you and can't wait to see you again. I thought it would be nicer for her to be able to hear my voice instead of just seeing my handwriting. Jay came to relieve me at midday, and he was well pissed off. Staff Large must've given him shit over something.

"What's up la?" I quizzed him.

"I fucking hate that fat twat. Who the fuck does he think he is?" Jay muttered angrily while I was still recording my message to Paula.

"Who's the fat twat Jay?" I asked knowingly.

"Fucking fatty Large. He's just given me loads of shit because the trailer came off the Rover and the leg on the trailer bent when it hit the ground. It wasn't my fault. Large's given me five extra duties has well.

If he says anything to me later about it, I'll punch the fucking cunt," he explained in rage.

I was quite sure, for I saw steam coming out of his ears and nostrils. As I left him, he told me that Sergeant B.J. wanted to see me.

16

I went in the back of Node Command, where Sergeant B.J. was sitting. He was tall man with a slender build that wore glasses with dark hair and scruffy moustache, and as soon as I got in there, he started to kick off on me audaciously over the state of my 1 Tonnie.

"You should be ashamed of yourself, leaving your det in that state. You are a detachment commander, and you shouldn't have left it like that!" He said with accusation creeping into his voice and then screaming with in a nirvana type of attitude.

"Erm, wait there a mo. I haven't been able to work on me rover for the last few days. Me rover has been out all over the show; plus, it's not me that leaves it in shit state. It's the people who have been using it lately, ok!" I screamed back at him.

He pissed me off, and after that little argument with the dickhead Sergeant, I thought, "The first chance I get to shoot him, I will."

I stormed out of Node Command and went straight over to my Rover to clear it out before I got in the shit again. When I opened up the side door of my 1-Tonnie, I could see what and why Sergeant B.J. was going on about. There were sweet wrappers, empty coke cans and mud all over the place. After seeing the mess, I tracked down the people, who last used it, and I made them clean it up. I wasn't going to clean their shit up. Once they had cleaned the 1-Tonnie out, I cracked on with the daily maintenance. There was no oil left in the engine, and one of the battery cells was bone dry. I was really fuming now because before anybody took a vehicle out they were dutifully meant to do a first works parade, which consisted of checking all of these levels.

Nevertheless, I was given a driving detail to pick Dave, a Relay lad, up from the dentist at Camp 4. As I drove down the MSR towards Al Jubayl, there was a convoy of British wagons carrying artillery shells, and the convoy was travelling North in the opposite direction in which I was travelling. After I picked Dave up, we started to drive back to our location. Excitement arose within me seeing the convoy of wagons again; in addition, it gave me a bit of an adrenalin rush and I wanted the war to kick off. We overtook the artillery convoy that I saw on my way to Camp 4, only this time we were also heading north, as was the convoy of trucks.

There was a phone run on tonight to Camp 4, so I put my name down on the list right away. I only had the one phone card, but it would be well worth getting down there to use it. A phone card lasted a lousy four minutes; that was all, but those four minutes was all I needed to hear Paula's voice, and to tell her that I loved her. There were plenty of phones in Camp 4, but only a few were in working order and there were always queues at the phones. Finally, I got through to Paula, and she was speechless when she heard my voice. Even though she was on the other end of the line, I couldn't think of much to say with writing bluey's to her every day. We exchanged our love for one another, "I love yeah and be careful," she said.

"I love yeah too. Don't worry. I'll be home in a few months," I said to reassure her.

The journey back was quick, and I went straight to bed with thoughts of Paula.

I awoke the next day, and found out that the medics from the RAMC had come into our location this particular day to give us all a couple of injections. One of the injections we got protected us against Anthrax and we needed to receive four Anthrax injections in total in order to protect us, for Saddam was prone to leash off a bombardment of chemical warfare that could contain the Anthrax virus. A pinhead amount of the Anthrax agent was all it took to kill us. The other one was a Pertussis injection, which would protect us from any bacterial weapons that Saddam would want to attack us with. We would need to have three of these injections. I broke out in a sweat when I saw the needle. Ever since I had gotten that Cholera jab back in Germany, I hated needles because a couple of the hours after receiving the Cholera injection, it had an adverse affect on me, and I collapsed feeling feverish, which lasted an intense twenty-four hours.

The medic did a good job and kept my mind off my bad thoughts and fears of the injection while he pierced my arm with the needle and emptied the contents of the syringe into my arm. I felt the watery sweat that started to appear on my forehead, as the fluid from the syringe moved round my body. I was over the moon when it was all over. However, in a sadistic tone the medic said, "There's more to come but not yet. Later on".

When the medic finished, he gave me a piece of paper that was a temporary Certificate of Vaccination, containing the dates of when I had

My certificate of injections, Saudi Arabia, January 1991.

received my injections and the dates of when I was due for my next injections.

Once everyone had been given their jabs, we were told to line up in front of Captain Carey, the squadron 2i/c (*second in command*), who was sitting behind a table in the admin tent waiting to issue us with this month's water money. Everyone from an officer down to the lowly rank of Signalman got paid the same amount, 1,050 riyals. When converted into sterling, the monetary units worked out to be about £150. £150 was a lot of money out in the middle of the desert. I put some money away in my Post Office savings account for whenever there was a Royal Engineers field Post Office about. The rest I had blown on sweets cans of lemonade and gambling. We bought the sweets by the box and cans by the slab. Also, it came in handy being paid that day because there was a CSE (*combined services entertainment*) show on that night in Al Jubayl.

Sergeant B.J. drove a load of us to Al Jubayl in a 110 Land Rover. He was a shit driver like one of those people who thought they knew everything about anything, but, actually, Sergeant B.J. didn't know jack shit. We all took the piss out of him, and the Sergeant was the butt of all our jokes. Sergeant B.J. must have been raging because every time he went to open his mouth we shot him down in flames with our witticism,

79

and the reason we ripped him apart so much was because he was such a miserable bastard.

As soon as we were all inside the building, Sergeant B.J. called us all over to sit by him like a school teacher trying to keep control of his pupils out on a day trip, but we were no school kids. "Fuck off!" One of the lads shouted, as we all scarped away from him and sat where we wanted to sit.

The hall soon filled up, and it was choker when the show had begun. First up on the stage was a young comic. He was good and humorous, and everyone laughed hysterically at his jokes. Secondly, an ex R.A.F. bloke came on, who was dressed in boots, tropical combats, a shirt and an old fashioned R.A.F. flying jacket. He looked familiar and then it dawned on me where from. I remembered seeing him on the tele when I was younger. His act consisted of an impressionist. He did aircraft impressions and was good at it. His best impression was of a Spitfire plane from the Second World War. Thirdly, the comic Mike Miller came on, and he had me in stitches all the way through his act. I hadn't laughed so much in all my entire life. Finally, once his act was over, a young vivacious lady singer came on the stage, and she was gorgeous. The crowd went wild with lust. All of the wolf whistles were so deafening; granted we couldn't be blamed for our reactions because she was dead fit. She graced the stage wearing a tropical combat uniform, and her hair was long, dark brown and curly. I thought she was half cast. After a few songs, she started a striptease by slowly unbuttoning her shirt, teasing and tantalizing us as each button popped off. Under her shirt was a black top, which covered her whole body, along with her arms and neck. The crowd screamed even louder. Once her shirt was off, she turned her back on us and pointed her bum in our faces, and that sent us off our heads screaming for more. All the derogative remarks about what we would like to do to her in that position came flowing out. This was a definite treat for us all to enjoy. She continued to strip; teasingly lowering her combats and making the crowd grow frantic as if they never saw a woman before. Once she had stripped further, she revealed a tight fitting black cat suit. She had one hell of a curvaceous figure on her with all the curves in all the right places. Looking round, I could picture all the lads as they drooled down their chests. The wolf whistles grew louder and louder. The bloke on my right hand side, who was from the medics, shouted at the top of his voice, "Get your tits out for the lads!"

Unfortunately, she didn't hear him because she seemingly looked as if she had a decent set of top bollocks on her. When the noise died down, she asked for a volunteer to join her on the stage.

No sooner had she spoken those words a chubby Scottish bald lad jumped up on the stage to join her. "How long have you been over here?" She asked him.

"Three days," he replied in excitement.

"Three days. You'd think you'd been here three months by the way you're going on," she teased him.

They sung the song *I'm so excited* by The Pointer Sisters. Every time it came to the line *I'm so excited*, the Jock would scream it out at the top of his voice. He was a game for a laugh and when the number had finished, the show organizers couldn't get him off the stage for ages, but he eventually jumped off the stage on his own free will. She was the last act on the show, which was pretty disappointing because it was the best time I've had while I'd been here. The singer left us all on a high sensational enchantment, boosting our morale and taking our minds off of the war for a night. The whole show was fairly fabulous with a broad range of acts but not one topped the singer. We returned back to our location late that night, and when we saw the rest of the lads, we told them that there would be another show the following night.

17

The next day came promptly, however, there wasn't much on work wise, and because of this, I had the perfect opportunity to write some bluey's back home. The excitement lingered in me from the show I saw the night before. The admin tent was loaded with lads, scribbling away with pens and papers. Life was pretty boring at this moment over here. To be specific, the lads even wrote to people they didn't really like just to receive mail back from those people. Receiving letters from back home thrilled us all and gave us an opportune moment of pleasure, which was rare; in addition, we all looked forward to getting those letters out of the mailbag, and to hear our names being called in the admin tent when the mail came. I had been receiving quite a few letters from Paula lately, mainly all sloppy ones; still I enjoyed them all the same. It was great to know someone at home was waiting for me on my return. Consequently, Paula wasn't doing too well. Life wasn't all that great in Paula's house at that particular time. I sent a cheque for £10 in a bluey to me mother, so she could buy Paula a flower arrangement for Valentines Day next month from me. Just as I'd finished licking my last bluey down, Lieutenant Naden came into the admin tent, peered directly at me and told me to get his Land Rover ready.

I still hadn't got to know Lieutenant Naden all that well, but he did seem to be alright. While we've been over here, we'd had a bit of a laugh with him. I thought this was because he was only a young man in his early twenty's. A suitably academically qualified person only has to be eighteen years old to enlist as an officer cadet at the Royal Military Academy Sandhurst with their training lasting forty four weeks comprising of three terms. My personal opinion on the age of officers in the army when they first enlist should not be eighteen, but should be at least twenty-five when they start their cadet course, for an individual at that age had much more maturity and skills to look after the welfare of a troop or a unit of men in a combat zone. In spite of his age, Lieutenant Naden did not do a bad job at all as troop OC.

I drove Lieutenant Naden to Trunk Node 043's location, which was situated thirty minutes further north up the MSR. When we got close by, we drove up a steep sandy hill to actually get into the heart of 043's location. Their location was situated on a plateau over looking the MSR.

We had to come to 043's location to verify a grid reference where we would RV (*rendezvous*) with a couple of Relay dets. While Lieutenant Naden went into 043's Node Command, I would have the chance to see some of the lads I knew and hadn't seen since we left our last location, such as Scouse Robbo and Greeny, and they told me what had gone on a few days previous with Greeny. A Bangladeshi Army unit was located at the bottom of 043's location, and a delegation of Bangladeshi Officers made a visit to 043's location in order to introduce themselves whilst Greeny was staging on. The lads told me that one of the Bangladeshi officers asked 043's OC whether they had women in their location or not. 043's OC informed the Bangladeshi officer that they did not have any women in their location, but the Bangladeshi officer informed 043's OC that they did have women as the Bangladeshi officers passed one on the gate when they entered the location. The Bangladeshi's had certainly mistaken young Greeny for a young girl, and 043's OC had to explain that it was not a girl but a young lad. This didn't matter to the Bangladeshi officer Scouse Robbo informed me because they still wanted to trade their army desert camouflage uniform for Greeny. I hilariously started to laugh out loud at the thought of Greeny getting used as a 'rent boy' by the Bangladeshi's. Furthermore, Scouse Robbo informed me that when the rest of the lads heard about what the Bangladeshi's wanted with Greeny, they took the piss out of Greeny, telling him that they were going to tie him to a Land Rover tailboard and sell his arse for 10 riyals a go. I burst aloud into more fits of laughter, but Greeny was not too impressed as with being a young 17-year-old naïve teenager, he actually thought the lads were serious.

After about twenty minutes, we received the verification of our next grid reference. We travelled for about another hour and half further north, along the MSR following the map that Lieutenant Naden had in his hands. We drove through a town and past a SPAM location.

"Right Molloy, there's a right turn coming up. I want you to take that turn. It'll put us on a desert track."

"Yes sir," I replied.

I turned right onto the desert track and drove into the desert by-passing another SPAM location. The SPAMs had loads of troops on the ground over in the desert because we often caught glimpses of them all and their trucks and their tanks, and their Air Force's planes that flew high above and their helicopters that flew much lower to the ground, both drilling daily routine sorties. By the amount of SPAM troops that I saw in Saudi, I thought that in any unlikely event of America getting invaded, they would be defenceless and in deep shit. Up ahead of us I noticed a couple of familiar wagons, and they were Relay wagons we were to RV with.

"I want you to pull up by the relays," Lieutenant Naden ordered me.

"Yes sir," I replied, as I pulled up by the wagons.

The wagons were only about five minutes away off of the MSR.

Captain Cary turned up on his own, to RV with us at the Relay wagons location to give Lieutenant Naden a new grid reference to where we would be taking the Relay wagons. Once Lieutenant Naden received the new grid reference he got out his Magellan GPS (*Global Positioning System*), to show the 2i/c. The Magellan was a brilliant piece of a kit. The GPS worked by satellites in space, and it helped us to pin point where we were on the ground within a few meters, it was a very high-tech piece of kit. To use the GPS, we simply typed in which position we needed, and the GPS sent a signal to a satellite and cross-referenced it with other satellites. We could not do without a GPS over here in the desert, because all the maps were generally useless. For example, being in the desert, we might as well have just brought over sheets of sandpaper and tried to work from them. The Magellan even told us how to get to a particular grid reference, and that was the importance of the GPS to us in all of our locations. Captain Carey was impressed with Lieutenant Naden's new toy and after he had finished playing with it, he went over to the Relay dets to inform them they were being deployed to a new location. The Relay wagons dropped their shots and started to de-cam (*remove camouflage*) their wagons ready to move.

"What's up, sir?" I curiously asked Lieutenant Naden.

"We're off to 012's location in order to drop off these Bedford's," he muttered back whilst his head was in his map and punching the grid reference into the Magellan GPS.

After the short meeting with Captain Cary, and then once back on the MSR, following Lieutenant Naden's navigation, we carried on further north with the Relays wagons in tow. It wasn't long before Lieutenant Naden indicated for me to turn left onto the desert between the rows of telephone masts. Then, I indicated a left turn in order to let the Relays know we were pulling off into the desert. There looked to be a very small town on the right hand side of the M.S.R. It didn't look like a big town. There was a row of concrete buildings with scruffy looking shops on the ground floor with homes above them and a few cars parked outside the shops. The town spread beyond the shops by a few rows of buildings. The desert was hard and flat, which was good, as we picked up some decent speed. The faster we went the greater the dusty clouds arose behind us.

The short journey took us about ten minutes to reach 012's location. Only one Relay wagon would stay at 012's location, and we took the other one to another location. Dusk gradually came upon us as we headed for the next location. When we reached the MSR, we did a steady one hundred kilometers an hour, this time heading south. Darkness had fallen and the nightly blackness was beginning to fill the sky. I indicated a right at the lights, which the streetlights brightly lit the street and the surrounding areas on both sides of the road. Just ahead of us, about one hundred yards from the traffic lights was a Saudi Civil Police roadblock. As we approached the roadblock, one of the police officers waved us through, and so we thanked him as we passed. The road led to a town that was very quiet and hardly had any traffic on the road. There was a roundabout at the beginning of the town, where I turned left, carried straight on passed some buildings on my right hand side and into the desert, and all of a sudden the night turned pitch black with only the lighting coming from the headlights of the Land Rover. As soon as we hit the desert at the back of the town, Lieutenant Naden ordered me to kill my headlights and turn to convoy lights. It was a struggle to drive without any lights, and, therefore, I drove moderately and dawdled my way through the darkened desert. The only light available to me was the moonlight and the light from the stars. The ground was extremely bumpy, and I felt as if I was on a fairground ride with the Land Rover getting shaken about. Ahead, I noticed a pinhole of a light at the top of a hill.

"What's that light up there?" I asked Lieutenant Naden.

"I think that's where we'll be dropping off this Bedford," he replied whilst he checked our position on the Magellan.

As we approached the light, it grew bigger and brighter until we saw a silhouette of squaddie. As soon as I came to a halt, Lieutenant Naden jumped out of the Land Rover and went over to the light, and, shortly after, Lieutenant Naden returned to the Land Rover and got back in.

"Right, Molloy. This is the place. We're leaving the Bedford at their guard post, and then let's get back to our location," he schematically told me.

Hence, we dropped the Bedford off; I turned the Land Rover round and went back out the same way we came in. It was pretty late when we returned back at our location, but I enjoyed the day out and it was a break from the monotonous camp routine. After dropping Lieutenant Naden off by Node Command I parked the Land Rover up in the Rover Park, and headed straight for the admin tent to check if I had any mail. There was no mail for me, so since I was tired I headed straight for my doss bag.

18

The rainy season started this month, January, and our location became so muddy that nobody ventured out of their tents or wagons except for meal times, mail times and staging on. I felt the same, for the raindrops were like artillery shells falling from the sky. Luckily, I brought my waterproofs with me and did not pack them in my MFO boxes back in Germany. The majority of the lads didn't bring their rain gear with them, and a few of them even took the piss out of me back when I packed mine in my kit. "You won't need them where we're going, Scouse. We're off to the hot dry desert?"

"Yeah never know, la," I answered.

I was always ready for anything, and as a result, it paid off for me being a smart arse on this occasion. Lieutenant Naden called me into Node Command, and he told me to get his Land Rover ready because he needed to go to the field hospital.

On our way, along the MSR in the direction of Al Jubayl, there had been a traffic accident. There was a huge SPAM truck, which was equivalent of one of our Bedford wagons, with its entire front end totally smashed in; moreover, the remains of a SPAM jeep, which now resembled a matchbox toy car as both lay demolished on the ground. The ones in the jeep were sure to be dead. No one could have survived that sort of crash. Since the SPAMs have been over here, they had had loads of road traffic accidents. I reckon they must have lost about fifty blokes up to now, and the war hadn't even started yet. The traffic accident didn't hold us up too much, so we continued on the field hospital.

As the rain still came down by the bucket loads, we arrived at the field hospital. The area around the field hospital was very wet, muddy and slippery. As I drove around the field hospital, I felt like I was participating in the Lombard RAC rally. I had the Rover in 4-wheel drive, but I was not getting anywhere fast. The more revs I put on the engine the faster the wheels just spun round, gaining no traction whatsoever. I can't say I didn't enjoy it because when Lieutenant Naden got out, I drove around again, twice, having some fun whilst I waited on the Lieutenant, who came back after about half an hour later, and he didn't say what was the matter with him, so we made our way back to our location.

On the return trip back to our location, I headed straight for the admin tent to see who was up to what. Inside the semi-lit tent were Jay, Flinnie, Sam Marriott and Mick Duggon. They all sat around the latest issue of the *Forces Echo*, searching through for pen pigs. The *Forces Echo* was the equivalent to a tabloid newspaper just for the British military forces. I got myself a bluey and joined in to help improve our pig board. I was about to give up when one girl caught my eye. She was from over the water in Wallasey, and her name was Sharon. I wrote and told her I was from Liverpool and asked her if she ever came over to our side of the water on the ale. Wallasey is on the Wirral peninsula, which is situated on the other side of the River Mersey to Liverpool. When Scousers referred to people from that part of Merseyside, it was always 'from over the water.' We real Scousers knew people from 'over the water' as 'Plastic Scousers,' for they liked to portray themselves as real Scousers, when in fact they are not. In addition, I told Sharon I supported Everton Football Club and also what kind of music I was into, such as the Liverpool band *The Farm*. I asked her what was happening back home, so I wasn't missing out on too much. The reason I wrote to her was not to be disloyal to Paula in anyway, but for the specific purpose that she was a local girl; in addition, she was someone else that I could get more mail from. I needed as much mail as I could get if even from a pen pig, when I was stuck in places like this desert.

The vast majority of pen pigs are ugly and can't get a boyfriend. Some of the cheeky bitches even stipulate from which particular ranks they wanted replies from, such as officers, senior NCOs or junior ranks. The pen pigs, who asked for further up the chain of command, were after a meal ticket. Nearly, every army unit that went away for long periods of time, set up these pig boards, for it was good for their morale.

We spent all afternoon and evening writing bluey's. I received a bluey from one of my mates Mick Houghton. He was from back home and he told me how Everton was doing, and he seemed like he was high on pot or intoxicated on something has he wrote this bluey, because his writing wasn't his usual neatness. As always, I wrote back and asked what else was up and called him a druggie, as he and the rest of my mates were always going to the clubs and illegal raves popping Ecstasy tablets and LSD (*lysergic acid diethylamide*) trips. It seemed a bit hypocritical of me calling Mick a druggie, for before I joined the army, I had a little experiment with smoking pot and popped a few LSD trips. I think most

Jay writing a bluey to a pen pig.

teenagers experiment in drugs at some stage in their life, which may be due to either peer pressure or just being rebellious. I know if I hadn't have joined the army when I did, that I would have been just like my civvie mates back home still experimenting with drugs. Once I posted my bluey's, I made my way over to the Rover Park to get my 1-Tonnie as today was my turn to visit the field hospital.

Andy drove me to visit the field hospital to see the dentist. I had a chip in the right corner of my upper front left tooth that happened when I bit into an apple, and the roughness on my tongue was doing my head in. I didn't have to wait long to be seen, unlike the NHS (*National Health Service*). The dentist was an officer and was sound, even though he came from Manchester. He told me that he had spent a little time at the Liverpool Dental Hospital a few years back. The dental hospital is where they train all the dental students in Liverpool. I went there a couple of times as a kid for dental treatments. Lying on a medical table, I didn't feel a thing as he slowly pushed the needle into my gum, numbing it with its contents. Has soon as my gum was totally numb, it took him about five minutes for him to sort out my tooth. When I came out of the tent, Andy was waiting to take me back to our location.

Tea was being served back at our location on our return, and I also found out that we were making another telephone trip that evening. After tea, I jumped on another phone run to Camp 4, even though I hadn't any phone cards left, I knew that I would be able to buy one in the shop there. Paula wasn't in when I phoned her, so I didn't use my entire phone card. In addition to using the phones, we had time to go to the PX shop at the port.

The PX was the American force's equivalent to the British forces NAAFI, which were both equally important, but the American's were better and cheaper. The SPAMs got well looked after by their government, while we just got used and abused by ours. When we got there, they also had a burger bar wagon next to the tented PX shop. I couldn't believe my eyes when I saw it. Only the SPAMs could go to war with a burger wagon in tow. Whilst Flinnie and I stood in the queue to the PX shop, a SPAM came over and asked Flinnie excitedly, "Do you mind if my buddy takes a photo of you and me together? I just love that beret?"

"Yeah why not." Flinnie replied.

When the photo shoot was over, they couldn't thank Flinnie enough. The SPAMs could be right dickheads at times.

Before returning back to our location, we thought we would give the phones another shot at Camp 4, because we didn't know when we would get our next chance. We didn't have to wait that long for a phone, which made a change. Flinnie got on the phone next to me and pulled out a great big stack of phone cards. I had a couple phone cards myself that I had purchased from the camp's shop, and this time when I called Paula, she was in, and we had a good chat. She was really missing me; loads I could tell by the tone of her voice. This situation between Paula and I really pissed me off, for I was over here instead of being in Liverpool with her. It was times like now that I really wished I wasn't in the fucking army. I would have given my right arm to be home with her now. Paula meant more to me than the army would have ever meant to me. The pips went on the phone to signal my money was running out, so we said our good byes and left me on a bit of a downer all the way back to our location. I laid in my doss bag and thought of Paula until I fell drowsily asleep.

The weather was far better, as I awoke the next day, unlike the rainy days we'd had, for the sun was shining brightly and after breakfast I grabbed the opportunity to do my dobhi. With all the bad weather we had experienced lately, everybody was unable to clean any of their uniform. I was coming up to my last pair of underwear and socks, and I didn't think Jim had done any washing since we've been out here. Persuasively, I got Jim to get his dobhi done, for his feet stunk like a bag of mouldy old spuds, and, sometimes I couldn't stomach the smells and odors in the confines of our dinky little tent whenever he took his boots off. And at times, I actually needed to walk outside the tent for fresh air. If it was not the Iraqis thinking about the use of gas to kill us, it was our own roommate with his raunchy stinking feet. Nonetheless, there was no need to be a fez (*someone who is not hygienic and festers in their own dirt*) especially over here. Once I had all my dobhi done and hung up to dry, I went and spent some trivial time doing first works on my 1-Tonnie.

The sun blazed so much that it was far too hot to do any work today, so, therefore, once I checked the 1-Tonnie's vehicle and radio battery acid levels, I went for a skive in the admin tent to give my Gat a good cleaning. Quite a few people were in the admin tent either writing blueys or cleaning their Gats too. I striped my Gat down for daily cleaning and laid all the parts out on the table. I hadn't actually adhered to the military discipline of daily cleaning rather my own discipline of weekly cleaning. When stripping down the SLR for a daily cleaning, the first parts of the weapon to be striped was the gas plug and rod, not any of the working parts yet. The reason for this being was that if you came under attack whilst cleaning your weapon, it was still possible to fire the weapon by cocking it for every shot fired. My Gat was caked with ample amounts of sand and dust, and if Staff Large had come in, I would have been given at least five extras (*guard duties*). I sat there for a moment and just looked around at everyone as they got on with whatever they were doing, but, still, I didn't think that it had sunken in yet that we may be off to war soon and may not be coming back. People treated the reality of this situation simply like an exercise, whereas, the reality was war and battles. While we were sorting out our personal admin, the Q entered the admin tent and placed a couple of mail sacks on the table by the tele that he brought back with him from Al Jubayl. I was starting to receive mail every other day now, which was a good thing

Today, the only mail I received was a letter from Ken Irwin. Ken was a mate from back home who I was in the cadets with. He was also in the Royal Signals, but with 202 Signal Sqn, which was based in Paderborn, Germany. Ken wrote in his letter that he had been posted up to 3 Div in to go on exercise. I thought that was mad since the Div and the majority of its vehicles were over here with us, far from Soest. Ken had also mentioned that there was loads of shagging that went on between the singlelies left behind in Soest, and the wives of 3 Div pads (*married soldiers*), as well as the wives of the Royal Jocks in Werl. I thought the wives must be right slags to do that on their husbands. It didn't come as a shock about the Royal Jocks wives shagging behind their husbands backs, as the wives of Scottish regiments were renowned within army circles for shagging about. I wrote back to Ken, informing him what I've been up to in the desert, which wasn't nothing much. I also took the piss out of him for being a war dodger, because he wasn't partaking in Op Granby. Ken told me in his letter that he and one of his mates had gone to Canada with the permission of the army to do a bit of skiing, but when they were due to come home, the pair of them had missed their flight, so another lad had to take his place. The lengths some people will go to, to avoid going to war I thought. I finished off the bluey by telling him not to get caught with a pads wife, but to enjoy himself all the same.

19

"Quick, get up. Sergeant Clay wants a word with everyone."
A nervous and anxious voice came from the tent doors and roused me awake. "Who's that?" I asked.
I was still half asleep, and there was no reply.
"Jim, Jay come-ed, we've got to get up. Fucking Sergeant Clay wants a word with us." I tiredly said while shaking the pair of them.
All three of us got ourselves casually dressed and made our way to the side of the admin tent, where the troop formed up in three ranks on parade. Sergeant Clay shouted at the stragglers to hurry up.
Once everyone was on parade, Sergeant Clay began to speak the tidings.
"Listen in lads. America has just bombed Baghdad. Just now at 3:00a.m. local time." There was coldness in his voice has those words came out.
I did not know how I really felt at that moment. My bottle went a bit in anticipation that we were about to be attacked and possible killed, and then, the adrenaline kicked in and started to race round my body with intense excitement, and my trained mind went into combat and warfare. All I thought about was fighter planes and bombers that were flying over our heads and would have dogfights with the Iraqi fighters. Also, I imaged artillery shells falling from the sky and dropping all around us; on one side, on the other side, behind us, in front of us, far from us, to the left and to the right, totally surrounding us, and we'd have to dodge them all as if in a slalom race.
The NBC alert was upgraded to stage two, and the guard was readied and doubled at each post. I donned my NBC suit, forgot about the unofficial army rule about not volunteering for anything and volunteered to stag on. I was on a tremendous hysterical high. My gut mainly hoped to see some action. The stag was a bore, and all we saw for the next two hours were the quick flashing lights that shone from the aircrafts thousands of feet in the air heading north to Iraq. The thoughts of peace were definitely wiped from my mind. The sun started to rise as my relief came to take over. I went straight to the tent and lay on top of my doss

bag to get an hour or so of sleep. I knew that once the SPAMs attacked with viciously purged bombardments like that - something I'd never seen before nor imagined, the war was on, and I needed to do my duties as I was trained to do.

This was the second day on the run now that we had good weather, and the sun cracked the flags. I couldn't think of a better climate to fight a war in. People carried on as if the bombs that were being dropped from the planes and the anti-aircraft fire from the Iraqis on the ground was all just a dream. I gave my Gat a good clean again especially as we were playing for real now. I'd have to discipline myself now to stay on top of my Gat and not let it get shitted up. One of the lads asked me to take him down to the troggy shop. I didn't mind, as I needed a couple of bits myself. On returning to our location from the shop, everyone ran around like headless chickens, trying to put on their NBC suits. I stopped the 1-Tonnie dead where it was, and we dragged our NBC suits out and got fully kited up. We learned that the NAIAD (*Nerve Agent Immobilised Enzyme Alarm and Detector*) alarm had gone off by accident, but we weren't about to take any chances. NAIAD was an automatic alarm system that continually monitored the surrounding atmosphere to provide audible or visual warnings of the presence of nerve agents in either vapour or aerosol forms. The equipment consisted of a detector and three remote alarms, which operate up to 500m away from the detector. NAIAD was a wet chemistry technology based on the enzyme cholinesterase. We stood round and watched the troggies work away in the quarry to see if any of them dropped dead. But, the troggies never did, so we took it as a gospel that it was safe to get out of the NBC suits and get back to normality, such as maintaining the Land Rovers, meals, staging on and receiving mail in the admin tent.

When the mail did come in, I received a bluey from Paula and a letter from my dad. I left the letter from Paula until later and opened the letter from my dad straight away. Inside was a letter from the taxman. I started to get nervous and slag them because I was at war and I thought these bastards were after me. My attitude soon changed when I opened the letter and inside was a tax rebate cheque for £213 and an accompanying letter stating that if I didn't agree with the amount, for me to return the cheque to them and they would asses my claim. Fuck that, I thought, and the cheque would go straight into my post office savings account the next time I'd be visiting Camp 4. If I was to send the cheque back to the Tax

Man, he would probably re-do his sums and keep hold of the money and there's no way I was going to let that happen. It brought a huge smile to my face, and I started to brag to the lads. They called me all the jealous words imaginable under the sun, although I chuckled in front of them all as I went to put my cheque somewhere safe.

After tea, I was sitting in the admin tent watching the same old videos when one of the Sergeants poked his head through the flaps of the tent. "Molloy. Outside a minute," he said hurrying me up.

I was very curious, for I knew I hadn't done anything wrong, but I went outside anyway. "Do you still want that American camp cot?" he asked.

"Yeah Sarge fucking too right. Oh, Jay Curly needs one as well," I replied with excitement.

"Right, there's a couple of Spams here from an engineer unit just down the road. Give me an army jumper and a pair of combat high leg boots, and I'll get you two brand new camp cots," the Sergeant said.

"Alright Sarge. I'll just go and get the kit for yeah."

I ran into our tent and told Jay what was happening, and he gave me the boots, and, then, I got my spare jumper and rushed them round to Node Command. I was given two camp cots still in the wrapper. The Americans' camp cots were another most sought out piece of kit by the British squaddie, because the frame was made from aluminium, very sturdy and was higher off the ground that the British camp beds. Because of this, it was comfy nights from now on. That night, Jay and I slept well on our new and more comfortable cots.

When I woke up the next morning, I realized that I'd been with Paula now for 17 months. The 18th of August 1989 was the first time I took Paula out, and that's when it all started. We've been through a lot together in that diverse short period of time. It just felt like last week that we first started to see each other. I'd never been out with a girl for more than six weeks before I met Paula. And after another delicious breakfast, I hurried back to my tent and wrote a couple of bluey's to Paula mainly to remind her of the date, but also to let her know that I hadn't forgotten. She was a sound girl, and I couldn't ask for a better girl to spend the rest of my days with. Once I'd finished my writing, Jim and I were sent on the rubbish detail.

I hated rubbish detail at times because my hands stunk of bad food, and it made me sick to my stomach, wanting to throw up. We took the trailer of rubbish down to the same usual place, where we always went to burn the rubbish. We made a pile out of the bin bags and emptied the water bowser on it. I poured petrol and diesel all over the bin bags, and Jim threw a match down to kindle it. In an instant, the bin bags went up in flames. I noticed a big pile of yellow aerosols that were just dumped there, and when I took a closer look, they were cans of fly spray. I reached down and picked some of them up, and the cans were full.

"Jim lets have a bit of fun," I told him with a sly deceitful grin on my face.

Jim and I knew it was a stupid thing to do, but it was sound at the time. I poured petrol all over the aerosols and put a match to them. Suddenly, that same whooshing noise was made when the cans blazed into flames, and the cans started to ignite one after another. Standing there still as a statue and watching the fires burn, took me back to when I was a kid. We used to go round and nick peoples rubbish out of their bin cupboards, and hoped that there were aerosol cans in them when we set them ablaze. What happened now was the mother of all rubbish burning. The cans blew up and flew across the nearby pile of rubbish and went on for about ten minutes. We took cover behind the Land Rover not to be hit by any low flying cans. They were loudly exploding about ten feet away in the air, and some cans even hit the Land Rover. Jim and I sat there pissing ourselves with laughter as we still took cover while more cans went whizzing over our heads. I was amazed that no one heard the explosions from the SPAM helicopter unit's location that was on the horizon to the front of us. Has soon as it was safe for us to come out of cover, with hastiness, we hooked up the trailer and made our way back to our location.

I spent most of the day at our location watching the bombers in the clear blue sky going to and coming back from the north. Somebody somewhere was getting a right malignant battering. I definitely would not like to be on the receiving end of all that bombardment. We watched as three fighter jets were escorting the bombers, and it seemed that the bombers were the American B-52's. All we saw when we looked up were the white bellies of planes. Even though the planes were so high up, we couldn't mistake the size of them. The excitement of the sight of the planes that flew at a very high altitude and going on their sorties of bombings soon wore off. One time when we saw the planes, the whole Node used to stop what they were doing and looked up. Now, it was just another added part of our normal lives out in the desert, and we all got used to the planes flying daily sorties over-head; moreover, the planes became boring for the fact of being a lowly Signalmen, who didn't get any reports on how successful, if at all, the bombing was.

20

Later on that day, Jim and I drove to where we saw the SPAM helicopter location, which we noticed on our last visit to the rubbish tip. The SPAM helicopter location was situated quite a few hundred yards beyond the rubbish tip and into the desert. We drove around the location for awhile to see if they had left any kit behind, which could come in use to the Node. After about a half an hour of driving, we came across a metal filing cabinet just lying on the ground. Driving the Land Rover, I pulled up next to the metal filing cabinet, switched of the Land Rover's engine, and both Jim and I jumped out of the cab. I reached for the handle of the top draw and began to open it inertly. I peered inside with curiosity to find it half-full of pens, pencils, rubbers and other bits of stationery equipment. The filing cabinet must have been in an admin tent in which the SPAMs couldn't take with them when they de-camped. There was stationery gear in the other draws that was more useful, "We can give all this shit to Staff Large. It might keep him off our backs for a bit," I told Jim.

"Scouse, what's that over there?" Jim said pointing behind us?

I looked over my right shoulder and there was a small dark square object on the side of a little sandy hill.

"Let's go over there and take a look. You never know," Jim said.

Once we had emptied the contents of the cabinet into the back of the Rover, we jumped back in our seats and made a beeline for the square object. When we arrived at the object, we noticed it had a dark green canvas cover on it. We both got out of the Land Rover to take a closer inspection. The canvas had "US ARMY" stencilled on it in black paint. Jim knelt down, took the canvas cover off it, and beneath the canvas laid a generator. The expression on our faces was one of disappointment because we had not found anything exciting. There was still a battery connected to the generator. We had no ability to test the battery to see if it worked or not. It must have been broken, and the cells in the battery must have been fucked too. Jim and I tried to lift it between us, but to no avail, it was way too heavy. "How the fuck are we going to get this back to our location?" Jim screamed.

"We'll come back later with Jay," I told him.

When we arrived back to our location, we gave Staff Large all the stationery kit we found and informed him and some others about the abandoned generator. "Take Jay Curly with you, and bring everything back here," Staff Large told us.

We grabbed hold of Jay and let him know what was happening. The reason why Staff Large told us to take Jay with us back to the generator was because Jay's trade is a Powerman and generators are his bread and butter. Therefore, the three of us drove back out to the generator. By the time we got back out from where we found the generator, it was dark. We only found it because we had the headlights on main beam, which shined brightly and lit up all the area in front of the Land Rover. Even with the three of us there, we still couldn't lift the generator. "It's no use. It's a heavy little fucker. We'll have to go back and grab about another ten pair of hands," I said to the both Jim and Jay.

So, we jumped back in the Land Rover and started to make our way back to our location. As I pulled away, we noticed a little Jerboa, more commonly known as a desert rat, which quickly hopped about on the desert floor in front of the Land Rover. I slowed down so Jim and Jay could get out. They started to chase after the desert rat, and it was dead funny to see those two lads running about the darkened desert chasing after the little rodent. I drove behind them trying to keep my headlights on the desert rat. It took those about ten minutes to catch up with the desert rat. That's the most PT those pair had done since being out here. I brought the Land Rover to a standstill and went to join them. However, before I got to them, they had already caught the desert rat and killed it. I didn't have a chance to save the terrified little desert rat. The headlights of the Rover shown down on the dead desert rat's corpse, and the desert rat looked like a cute furry little thing. Its fur was white on its belly and orange on its back, and on closer inspection, fleas were jumping about its fur.

When we got back, Staff Large enquired where the generator was. "You're going to need about another ten blokes to lift it," Jay told him.

It sounded better coming from Jay, for he was the Node's Powerman.

Therefore, Sergeant Clay grabbed another seven pair of hands, and we all climbed on the back of the POL wagon, including Sergeant Clay, and headed back out for the generator. We managed to lift it on the back of the wagon just about, but it was still very heavy even with all the hands we had on it. When we got back, we unloaded the generator, and, then, Staff Large told me that in the morning I would be taking Sandy to Trunk Node 012's location. Sandy was a VM (*vehicle mechanic*) from the

American Huey helicopter.

REME (*Royal Electrical and Mechanical Engineers*) attached to our Node as the Node's VM. His responsibility was to ensure that the Node's vehicles remained road worthy. Anxiously, I couldn't wait because that was another day out for me.

In the morning straight after breakfast, Sandy and I gathered what we needed for our journey to Trunk Node 012's location as we knew we would be out for best part of the day. Trunk Node 012 was the Trunk Node that Lieutenant Naden and I dropped off one of those Relay wagons a few days previous. We travelled north towards Iraq again, so we ably saw an array of more troop movements. It was a long drive up there, just so Sandy could get some Land Rover parts of off their Q. The journey back was a lot more interesting because we got to see the build up of troops that were headed north. We pulled over by a SPAM convoy and took some photos. There were plenty of AH-64 Apache helicopters and Bell AH-1 anti-tank gunships flying nearly on top of our heads, and they were accompanied by medical Huey helicopters. I managed to get my camera out, and I took a few snaps. The Heuy's had their gunmen hanging half way out the opened side doors. And, that sight made me think that this lot of SPAMs had watched way too many Vietnam War films. There weren't many exposures left on the camera film, so I managed to use them up before we returned.

When I arrived back in our location, the word went about that a card school would be starting in the next ten minutes in the admin tent. So, I headed straight for the admin tent to join in the nights entertainment, just as soon as I wrote a letter to Paula first, enclosing the used camera film that I had finished off today. Then, Flinnie asked me if I wanted a game of pontoon, and I did, so, I grabbed a seat and got settled in. After a few hands, the game was changed to three-card brag. I didn't have a clue how to play this game, so I stayed out for a bit to get to grips with it. Serious money was changing hands, and I took this opportunity to join back in the card game. A few of the lads left the game because the stakes got a bit too heavy for them. There were four of us left in the game, Jay Curly, Flinnie, another lad called Jay and myself. Jay had lost most of his money, so he quit the game, and by this point, there was quite a few bob in the middle of the table. I had a good hand, so I thought, and the bet rose to one hundred riyals, and I already put over three hundred and fifty Riyals into this hand, and then, my money ran out. I wanted to carry on, but I didn't have the finances to proceed. I was well pissed off, seeing all my wages amongst that enormous pile of money in the middle of the table. Now, I knew it was all over for me, and I would be skint till we were given our water money next month. Jay Curly and Flinnie carried on for a bit longer, and the pot grew bigger and bigger. Jay had an ace high flush, and Flinnie had eight, nine, ten, and he laughed all the way to the bank. Jay was sickened, and I felt like crying. I thought Flinnie was a bad card shark, and I called him for everything. It wasn't nasty. He was just a lucky bastard. Flinnie sat there for about ten minutes counting his winnings saying, "Guess how much, lads? Just over fifteen hundred riyals."

He rubbed his hands together with a jocundity smile upon his face.

That was more than two hundred pounds that Flinnie had taken from us. I wanted to continue to see if I could recoup some of the money I had lost to Flinnie, but I had no more money left whatsoever. I asked Flinnie to lend us two hundred riyals until we received our next allotted water money. Like a good lad he obliged, and like a dumb dickhead, I carried on and played cards. This time, we played Pontoon and the game didn't finish till 3:00a.m. I still had two hundred Riyals left by the time I went to bed. We had fun, for what else could we do with our money besides playing cards, but spend it on sweets and lemonade?

21

After going to bed in the early hours of this morning, I was still tired when I woke up the next day. Grumpily, I just didn't want to get out of my pit (*bed*) this morning. I forced my legs out from inside my doss bag and placed my feet on the sandy floor of our tent. I reached into my army travel bag and brought out a clean pair of socks and boxer shorts. There's no better feeling out here than being able to put on clean fresh underwear. I noticed that Jim was also getting out of his pit. He reached down for the same pair of socks that were stuffed deep inside his boots from the day before and put them on. With living in such close proximity to Jim, I knew he had put the same horrid underwear on for the past few days now. Jay and I emphatically shared the same opinion that Jim was a dirty fez bastard. Come to think of it, I couldn't remember the last time Jim had done his dobhi. Has we finished off getting dressed, Staff Large entered our tent and told Jay and I that we were to go on a driving detail.

Our detail was to try and find a chimney to fit the American burner that we had brought out with us from Germany. The burners were a great bit of kit for getting hot water. The heater went into a metal dustbin, had a petrol tank connected to it, and inside was a little tap to adjust the flow of the petrol into the heater. To get the hot water, we had to light the drops of petrol. And for it to work properly, we needed the chimney; hence, that was our mission for the day. We called in to Wilkies tent to grab him to come with us. Wilkie was a Relay Op and on the same det as Flinnie. We climbed into the 1-Tonnie and headed in the direction of an old SPAM engineer location that was situated ten minutes away from our location to seek out a chimney. As I turned right off the dusty track, Jay noticed a huge stockpile of boxed water on our left-hand side. Thus, I drove the 1-Tonnie over to the middle of the boxes of water. All of us jumped out and were bewildered by the vast amount of water that was all around us. The boxes must have been here for a while, certainly through the past couple of weeks when we'd had all that rainy weather as the vast majority of the boxes were not in good condition. "The Spams must've just packed up and left all this behind when they went to their new location," I said to them.

"Well, we're out to find a chimney, not to get water," Jay reiterated.

We drove round for about a half an hour and still couldn't find anything that would measure up as a chimney. I decided to take a drive further out into the desert just in case there was a chimney or something of the sort out there. We did find something alright, but it wasn't a chimney, it was another explicit SPAM location.

"Drive over to their camp, Scouse," Jay expressed to me.

So, I put my foot flat down on the accelerator and speedily headed straight for the camp. I recognised this camp, for it was the same SPAM camp that Jim and I came across with Lieutenant Naden and Sergeant Clay a couple of weeks back when we were out on a recce for a new location and I'd ran out of petrol on the way back. There were two guards at the gate of their location, and both of them started to approach us as we drove closer. I halted the 1-Tonnie about ten feet away from their gate.

"Hey mate, yeah wouldn't have any spare chimneys for a burner by any chance would yeah?" I asked the guard in a nice and pleasant tone?

"No. We don't. But, there's another unit about three kilometres behind that might have one," one of the guards informed me.

"Cheers la," I thanked them.

Taking the guards advice, I drove in the direction he'd pointed and stayed on the track that skirted to the left, around a barbwire fence of the camp and carried on in the direction in which we were guided. I noticed a big sand rock hill to our left that reminded me a bit like the rocky hills in a cowboy film. As we came from the side of the hill; we noticed a load of green army tents about a three-quarters of a mile away in the distance.

"That looks like the Spam's over there," Wilkie said.

So, I headed straight for the SPAM location, making good satisfying speed on the almost flat surface. We drove straight into their location without even being challenged. There were no guards. And, there wasn't even a barbwire fence for protection. I left the 1-Tonnie nearby, where I thought the entrance of the SPAM location should have been, and we took a quick lucid look round. We noticed a burner, which was the same as ours, straight away by the cook's tent. A little skinny bald-headed black man came out of the cook's tent to see what we were up to.

"Yeah wouldn't have any of those chimneys spare would yeah?" I asked politely.

"Of course we do," he replied.

The man went off behind the back of his tent, and he came back out five minutes later, clutching two pieces of chimney, "Here you go," he said has he handed the parts over to Jay.

By this time, his Master Sergeant, which was equivalent to our Sergeant Major, came over to see what was going on.

"Can I help you guy's?" He asked us.

He took his sunglasses off and cleaned them with a handkerchief.

"We came for some chimney parts that one of yeah men has kindly said we could have," I nervously told him.

Trying to keep a stern and calm look about - whilst Jay and Wilkie remained silent and left me to do all the talking; indeed, on the inside I thought we'd be in the shit for just turning up inside their location and asking for kit. All of a sudden, the Master Sergeant said, "Is there anything else I can help you guys with?"

"Yeah. There is something yeah might be able to help us out with. Is there any chance of getting us some camp cots?"

"Yeah. How many do you want, three?"

"We could use about five of them. But, whatever you have would be greatly appreciated," I replied.

"Yes. No problem. Come back tomorrow, and I'll have five cots for you to pick up," he said with a smirk.

I thanked him for his generosity, and we climbed back into our 1-Tonnie and happily made our way back to our location. On the way, we stopped off at the stacks of boxed water we saw on our way. We hopped out of the 1-Tonnie and managed to fit fifty-two boxes of water into the side and the back of the 1-Tonnie. "What are you going to do with all this water, Scouse?" Wilkie asked in bemusement.

"I'm going down to that troggy shop by the MSR and trade them in for some slabs of Pepsi," I told him as I slyly winked to Jay.

Once we had loaded the best conditioned boxes and secured them in the 1-Tonnie, we jumped back in and raced off to the troggy shop in the hopeful task of doing a Jesus Christ, but instead of changing water into wine I would be changing the water into Pepsi Cola. When we got to the troggy shop, I called the assistant out to have a look at all the water I had, "Hello my friend. How would you like to trade all this water for some Pepsi?" I asked him.

"Okay. Okay," he replied without any delay.

We shook hands on the deal, and I was on the upside, for I had what he needed.

"How much Pepsi would you like?" He asked.

We haggled a bit, and, then, we came to an agreement of ten slabs. All three of us unloaded the water, stacked it at the side of the troggy shop, and then collectively stacked the slabs of Pepsi in the 1-Tonnie.

Whilst heading to our location, I told Jay and Wilkie that I would take another trip there in another week or two. We were pissing ourselves with laughter at the little scam we just pulled off. "Just wait till all the other lads hear about this," I told Jay and Wilkie.

And, we carried on laughing all the way back.

22

When we arrived at our location that day, I drove straight to the admin tent to unload our spoils for the day, Jay went straight to see Staff Large, taking the chimney parts to give to him, and, then, Jay came back looking angrily pissed off. "What's up Jay?" I asked him.

"That ungrateful fat cunt didn't even say thanks for the chimney parts," Jay exclaimed.

I passed Jay a slab of Pepsi to take into our tent for our own personnel consumption whilst I took the rest into the admin tent for the other lads, "Bloody hell Scouse, where did you get all that from?" One of the lads asked me.

"You know how it is out here, a bit of this and a bit of that. I traded some boxes of water with the troggies," I explained as if I was Arthur Daley from the ITV television programme, 'Minder.'

Once I'd unloaded the Pepsi, I parked the 1-Tonnie in the Rover Park and went to trace Flinnie, for the debt I had with him.

Flinnie was staging on when I caught up with him, "All right Flinnie la, yeah just the person I've been looking for," I shouted with a small chuckle and wide grin.

"What can I do for yeah, Scouse?" Flinnie asked in wonder.

"Yeah know that two hundred riyals I owe yeah? What would yeah say if I could get me hands on a SPAM camp cot?" I asked with lucrativeness on my mind.

Enduing him with a rare SPAM camp cot, I hoped that he would knock about one hundred riyals off my debt from the last card school.

Wanting to collect his debt, Flinnie assured me, "If yeah can get me a camp cot, I'll forget about the two hundred riyals you owe me."

Unknowingly, he must've thought that I couldn't come up with the goods, whereas I had already acquired the deal to get the cots. Lingering about, I turned my back on him and steadily headed back with a slight grin on my face, thinking easy bastard.

When I got to the admin tent, I found out about another card school that was back on tonight as one of the local entertainments. Obviously, I hadn't learnt my lesson from my last experience and joined in with the usual crowd for a card game. A few of the lads took up the challenge and wrote to some pen pigs to kill their time, and some of the other lads played 'Risk' and other board games while others watched videos. As night fell, I went to play at the card school, and we played Pontoon through the night. I ended up with the same amount of money at the end of the night that I started with at the beginning. It got to the early hours of the morning again, and I was tired; therefore, I said my good nights and got myself off to bed. I was the first one to leave, but I managed not to get into debt this time.

The next morning, Jay, Wilkie, Sam and I went off to visit our friendly SPAM location to pick up the promised camp cots. When we arrived at the SPAM location, the Master Sergeant wasn't there, but he was true to his word as the camp cots sat on the ground beside one of the tents waiting for us. We stayed there for a bit talking to a few of the SPAMs. They were impressed with our 1-Tonnie, and they let us go into their jeep called a 'HMMWV.' I climbed inside the HMMWV, which was spacious compared to my 1-Tonnie. We took a load of photos with a SPAM and the HMMWV before we left. Jay and Sam had a look in a tent and came out with a couple of American medals that would have been awarded to American soldiers for 'Outstanding Military Achievement.' In addition, Jay robbed a SPAM desert camouflage hat that was tied to the jeep. He got his knife out and cut the hat off before any SPAMs noticed him.

I thought Jay and Sam were out of order, and they called us Scousers thieves. The SPAMs had been good to us, indeed, they welcomed us and didn't have to go out of their way either, but they did. If they had gone into a British Army camp and asked for kit, they would have well been fucked off. The British wouldn't part with the steam off its own shit. We wouldn't have given anyone anything unless we swapped it for something else like before with the water and Pepsi at the troggy shop. I thanked the SPAMs for the cots, and we left their location before they realized anything else was missing. If the SPAMs saw anything missing other than the cots, they probably would have started to shoot at us, so we wasted no time in getting out of there. When we returned, I gave Jim and Flinnie a camp cot each and let the rest of the lads fight over the other three cots. I was made up now because my debt with Flinnie had been repaid; moreover, at the end of the month, I was going to be two hundred riyals better off. The day was going good for me so far, and meeting with the SPAMs had definitely paid off.

The Q had brought the mail in today, so once I gave the cots away, I headed straight to the admin tent. The mail was given out in the admin

SPAM, me, Sam and Jay on a visit to a SPAM location for kit.

tent after tea, and there was a parcel for me. The parcel was from my mother. It wasn't much good and only filled mainly of two penny sweets, but the thought was good, and it reminded me of when I first joined the army in 1987, and my family used to send me sweet parcels through the post. Furthermore, I received a letter from Paula, and it was a sloppy one. I was too tired to write back tonight with the previous night's shenanigans in card school. Therefore, tonight was an early night, and I turned in for a good nights rest, for it had been a long day.

I arose early the next day with the sun off in the horizon, and I and took another drive to the SPAM location, where we were at yesterday that I picked up the cots. The Master Sergeant was there this time, so I thanked him personally for the camp cots. He led me to his tent to give me some more kit. "Do you want some of our MREs?" he asked.

"Yeah too right," I replied gratefully.

MREs (*meals ready to eat*), are the Americans equivalent of our compo rations of food, but better. They came in a thick brown plastic package, containing one meal. In some of them, you could get a Spanish omelette, a chunk of boiled ham and bottles of Tabasco Sauce, along with packets of M&M sweets. The Master Sergeant gave me a box of the MREs. I knew these would come in handy when the big push came as I was preparing for war. In addition, the Master Sergeant brought out a bottle of mineral water, but inside the bottle was not water, it was home brew.

It was beige in colour, had raisins floating in it and tasted like wine. He gave me some yeast and told me to just add water, fruit, and sugar, and then leave it ferment in a dark warm place for a fortnight. I thanked him again for his generosity and made my way back to my location again with some goods.

Back at our location, I took the box of MREs over to the slop jockey's tent, so they could put the MREs away for when they would be needed when we went into Iraq. It is hard to predict what happens in war and there might not be enough time for the slop jockey's to prepare and cook the Node a meal, so the MREs will be a necessity. After I gave the slop jockeys the MREs, I popped my head into the admin tent to see if there was any mail. There was no mail, but the Q did bring our second and final set of desert combat uniform back with him from Al Jubayl. We were still minus the desert helmet covers and it looked as if we wouldn't be getting issued with them either. This didn't bother the senior ranks, for they had their desert helmet covers. They had their typical grandiose, I'm all right Jack, attitude when any of the junior ranks raised the issue of desert helmet covers. However, we were the ones, the junior ranks, who got the cots, the chimney parts, the generators and all the other extra things we would be able to use. Was it any wander the lads were pissed off with the senior ranks! I just let it go about the helmet covers and went about my own business to get more of the boxed water and take them to the troggy shop.

I went with Sandy in the POL wagon back to where the boxes of water were to pick some more water up. But, I didn't get as much this time because an ample amount of the boxes were still ruined with a few rainstorms we'd just had. Yet, we took the water back down to the troggy shop for some more Pepsi. The same assistant was at the shop when we got there, so I knew I had a good chance to swap the water.

"I've got some more water for yeah, mate," I called out.

He came out and had a look on his face that was one of amazement, "I'll give you six Pepsi," he offered.

I thought about it and agreed on that amount, even though I thought it wasn't enough, but I was there then and didn't want to have to go back. Sandy and I unloaded the water before we loaded the Pepsi. As this was going on, a voice from the behind me said, "Typical Scouser, always on the fiddle trying to make something."

I looked round to my left where I heard the voice coming from and saw two British squaddies on army motorbikes. They weren't wearing any insignias, so I couldn't tell which unit they were with. I chuckled and smugly told them, "Fucking too right" as I finished off loading the Pepsi onto the wagon. The two motor bikers shook their heads with disapproval as they fastened the chin straps of their helmets before mounting their motorbikes and riding northwards into the distance along the MSR. Sandy and I thanked the shop assistant for his business and we made our way back to our location.

As before with the Pepsi on my return to our location, I would take them into the admin tent and place one slab in my tent. That one was my commission for using my initiative and intellect to get the water and then swapping the water for the Pepsi. If it hadn't been for me, nobody would have had any free Pepsi. Everyone in the Node was made up with the Pepsi as it made a refreshing change from drinking bland mineral water. As I was stacking the slabs of Pepsi on top of each other, Staff Large came into the admin tent and informed me that he had a little job for me to do in the morning and I was to report to him first thing after breakfast.

After breakfast I went to see Staff Large and he asked me to take Tosh and some boxes of our ten men ration packs with me to the SPAM location to see if we could swap them for their MREs. This time it was different when I arrived at the SPAM location. One of their Captains was there this time, instead of their Master Sergeant. I introduced ourselves to the Captain and enquired about the possibility of trading our boxes of ten men ration packs for some boxes of their MREs. The Captain was made up and satisfied with our rations, so he was happy to trade some more MREs. I asked the Captain if he could get me some of their issue jungle boots, and I'd swap him for a pair of my combat high leg. He nicknamed me the Scrounger because I was always at their location trying to scrounge kit off of them.

"I'll get you a brand new pair of jungle boots if you can get me a pair of those boots you are wearing," he said pointing at my boots.

He wasn't interested in my British Army issued boots. However, he was definitely interested in the pair of civvie desert boots I had on at the time.

"Well, sir, it just so happens that I have a brand new pair in me wagon. What size are yeah?" I asked him.

"I'm a size eleven," he replied.

American sizes are one size bigger than ours, so it was my luck that both he and I were the same size. I pulled them out of my bag, and he tried them on. He was made with them and greatly satisfied with the exchange; thus, he went straight into his tent and brought out a brand new pair of jungle boots and a desert camouflaged Bergen cover.

"Here you go, scrounger. You can have this as well," he said whilst handing them over to me.

It got close to teatime, and I had to get Tosh back to our location to cook our tea. We thanked the SPAMs and shook their hands before we left. We got back in a flash, and I drove Tosh straight to the cook's tent to unload the MREs. Sergeant Clay and Staff Large stood by the admin wagon and looked at what we were unloading. They noticed that I had the desert camouflaged Bergen cover, so they started to quiz me on how I got a hold of it. Sergeant Clay and Staff Large started to call me a Jack bastard because I had the Bergen cover. Both of them said I didn't get anything for the lads. I thought they had nerve calling me Jack. Undoubtedly, Sergeant Clay and Staff Large are the biggest Jack bastards going, and most of the lads thought so too.

Angered and with a prerogative attitude, Staff Large said, "You're confined to camp now, Molloy!"

Just because I had a piece of kit that they didn't have, they confined me to camp. They must have forgotten about the camp cots and MREs that I managed to get my hands on, not to say the slabs of Pepsi, which was for the benefit of everyone. At least I could sleep at night and there weren't thirty plus Gats pointing at my back. I went to find Jay to let him know what Staff Large had just said to me.

On my way to find Jay, who was coming down from showers, I noticed a few more wagons had joined our Node and were parked up under camouflage nets by the Relay wagons. I asked Jay who did the wagons belong to and he informed me that they belonged to SEP (*System Executive Plans)* and they would be in our location for a few days. I did not know who SEP was or what job they done because with being a lowly Signalman it seemed that I did not need to know this information. While Jay and I walked back to our tent, I informed him what had just gone on with Staff Large and him confining me to camp. Jay shook his head in disbelief and I even told him that I was starting to get pissed off being in this Node.

23

As soon as breakfast was over on this overcast morning, I trudged around, managing to scrounge some fresh fruit from the slop jockeys for my home brew. I took a twenty-litre black water jerry can off my 1-Tonnie to make my home brew in, and the ingredients I used were: Six litres of water, eight ounces of yeast, two pounds of sugar, four small banana's, four apples and a handful of raisins, just like the SPAM Master Sergeant advised me. I filled the jerry can with all the ingredients and gave it a good shake to ensure all the ingredients were mixed together. I went to see Sam Marriott and Mick Duggon in their tech's Bedford and they made me a black plastic breather tube long enough to put one end over the small hole of the jerry can and the other end went into a bottle of water, allowing no air into the jerry can and let the gases out when the brew started to ferment. The sun was starting to break out of the clouds, so I placed the jerry can behind some rocks in direct sunlight to aid in the fermenting process. I'd do this every day now, and the brew would be ready to drink in a fortnight.

All of this hard work took me up to tea because I couldn't let any of the high almighty senior ranks know what I was up to, so I needed to be stealthy whilst working on my brew. Tea was lovely as usual; in addition, I had steak and kidney pudding, which in the army was called 'babies head.' With those, I also had boiled potatoes, carrots and cabbage. For dessert, I had apple crumble with custard, and it was out of this world. After tea, I caught up with some mail that was outstanding.

I wrote to my Nan and Granddad, and to Paula. In the bluey to Paula, I sort of wrote the words down in a madrigal way, using the words from the song *Unchanged Melody* by The Righteous Brothers. I thought that I must have been getting soft in my old age, writing down words from a love song. It took me most of the night to catch up on my mail. Once I finished, I packed away my writing material and bid the lads good night.

The next day, there was plenty of work in our location with the bad weather over the last few days. I was on cam-net duty, fixing the cam-nets on the Rover Park. It looked as if it was going to rain again that particular day with all the dark rain clouds overhead. The rain held off all day, so I engaged in a game of football that was on for that afternoon. About half of the Node turned up for the football match. We were divided into two teams, Admin lads versus the Relay lads. Whilst we enjoyed ourselves, having a good kick about, the SSM came around with a video camera. With the Admin lads winning the final whistle of the match went off at 3:30pm to give us all time to get a shower before tea.

The SSM also filmed everyone doing their daily jobs like manning the sets in the back of the wagons or maintaining the vehicles. Mainly, he filmed the pads so that they could send messages back home to their wives. He poked the camera's lens into our tent and asked Flinnie to say a few words to his wife. Flinnie froze and didn't really know what to say. I sat next to him and prompted him. He spoke like a robot in front of the camera. Then, the SSM turned the camera on me and asked me to say a few words to the lad's back in Soest. Has I sat straight up on my cot with my feet on the ground, I looked directly into the camera and explained how we saw the American B-52 Bombers. In addition, I talked about their escort fighter jets that flew along side the Bombers, under them and over them as well as in front and behind the Bombers, totally surrounding them on their sorties to Iraq and Kuwait. I'd never seen so many planes in my life. Furthermore, looking directly into the camera, I told them about our daily activities. I mentioned that in the evening we played cards while we waited for the mail to come in. I even said how much mail came in, which wasn't much at all, and I explained how we hoped we'd get more in tomorrow's mail.

The next day the weather was a lot better with the sun out and an array of odd shaped white clouds in the sky. I took this opportunity to crack on and did my dobhi before the weather changed again. I had a huge pile of dirty clothes because of the dirty and rainy weather over the past week. Jim only had a little dinky pile of clothes to be washed. He must have worn the same socks for about three days, and his feet half stunk. I had to get out of the tent every time he changed his socks. If Jim's feet stunk that badly, God only knows what his underpants were like. However, I tried to not think about that much whilst being confined to our camp, where I spent some of the time in my tent.

Even though I was confined to camp, I did manage to go with Jay and fetch some of the boxes of water in the 1-Tonnie. We stayed there for about a half an hour, loading water until we couldn't fit any more in the wagon. When we got back, Staff Large told us to take the water straight up to the showers and fill the tank up. When all the boxes were unloaded, Jay drove the 1-Tonnie to the Rover Park while I topped up the shower tank. Having the remaining boxes of water up at the shower, meant that we didn't have to traipse buckets of water up the hill when we needed a shower. While I was up at the showers I noticed that SEP were de-caming their wagons and packing away their tents. SEP had only been in our location for a few days and they were about to move to another location. When I finished with the water and showers, I spent the rest of the afternoon in the admin tent giving my Gat a good clean, for I've neglected it a bit lately. Staff Large brought in a new stag list and pinned it up in the admin tent. I left my Gat in bits on the table whilst I went over and inspected the new stag list. Unsurprisingly, there were no senior ranks on the list as usual. It's one rule for one and one rule for the other. This started to piss the lads off. And, the seniors really got on my nerves now. Looking at the stag list, I saw that I was on stag duty at 21:00 with Sam.

Sam and I were on prowl for two hours. The stag dragged on for ages with us; however, we had just a small area to patrol. The only interesting thing that happened was that we saw the planes heading north. I walked round with my head up my arse and thought about receiving some mail. There had been no mail for about four or five days, and everybody's morale started to hit rock bottom. Livening the stag up, Sam and I snuck up on the guard posts, but in the end we decided against that idea has we may have gotten ourselves shot. As soon as our stag was over, I headed straight for my pit. I couldn't wait for this day to be over because I had hit an all time low with a combination of the new stag list and not receiving any mail for days.

24

It was my turn for pan bash after breakfast, and I sharply cleaned all the greasy pots and pans. As well as staging on, there was also a rota for pan bash after every meal. The worst time to be on pan bash was after tea. I thought the slop jockeys purposely used every dish, pot and pan they could find just to piss us off. There wasn't that many pans after breakfast, so Jay and Jim gave me a hand, and we had it all done in fifteen minutes.

After cleaning all the dishes, we waited on the mail because today the mail came in for the first time in about a week. I expected to get loads of mail, but the only letter I got was from my mam and it pissed me off. She didn't have much to say, only about her shops. There wasn't any letters or parcels from Paula, and that upset me a bit. I grabbed a couple of blueys from the admin tent, replied to my mam's letter, and wrote to Paula to cheer myself up. Sergeant Clay saw me wearing the jungle boots I got from the SPAMs, and he said they didn't suit me. He was only jealous because he didn't have a pair. I just ignored the fat bastard and went to fetch Tiny for our stag.

Tiny and I had a laugh as we staged on together, taking the piss out of the senior ranks. Everything we said about them was true; they are a bunch of selfish bastards who only cared about themselves. Half way through our stag we were ordered to start taking our NAPS (*Nerve Agent Pre-treatment Set*) tablets again and to go into NBC stage 2, which comprised of wearing our NBC suits along with the NBC over boots, white inner gloves and black rubber out gloves that looked like domestic cleaning marigold gloves. I didn't know what had happened, but I followed my orders as I was trained to do. We had previously taken NAPS tablets when we were issued with them not long after arriving in Saudi and after a couple of weeks and for some unknown reason to me we were ordered to stop taking them. The NAPS tablets were issued to every soldier out here and we had to take one tablet every eight hours to help the bodies' immune system combat any nerve agent that Saddam may have wanted to unleash on us. The problem I had along with many of the other lads was when taking the NAPS tablets was that they made us lethargic and gave us headaches but we were ordered to take them. "I wander what's happened," Tiny said whilst he rubbed his chin.

"Someone has probably just done a really bad fart and the seniors are flapping." I told him as I pulled my NBC trousers up, got into my uncomfortable suit and unknowingly wondered what was going to happen.

When I finished my stag, Sandy came over, and he let me know that the four-wheel drive Propshaft on my 1-Tonnie had snapped off. I was well pissed off when Sandy told me that. I couldn't trust anyone to look after my equipment. I asked Sandy how long it would take for a replacement part to come in, "How long is a piece of string?" he oddly replied in wonder.

"Fucking great!" I screamed out in frustration.

I pictured myself in one or two months time pushing my 1-Tonnie through Iraq and on into Kuwait with Sergeant Clay at the helm giving his direct orders. I could still use it, but I didn't have four-wheel drive. I could drive it in two-wheel drive and hope I didn't come across any soft sand.

I went in the admin tent and watched the recordings of television programmes from the British Forces SSVC (*Services Sound & Vision Corporation*) channel back in Germany. I wrote a bluey to Mick, my druggie mate back at home, and I let him know what was happening over here. There wasn't much change since the last time I wrote to him a fortnight ago. I put his bluey in the mailbag, which would be ready for tomorrow, before I retired to my pit early that night.

I felt very pleased when the mail came in today as did everybody else. There were a couple of parcels and a few blueys waiting for me in the admin tent. One of the parcels was from my mam and the other from my dad. I opened the one from my mam first, which was a lot better this time from the previous one she had sent. There were plenty of Mars Bars and other different chocolate bars contained in the parcel. When I emptied the sweets out of the box, I noticed there were three video films at the bottom. When I read what was on the tapes, a huge grin came upon my face and my eyes opened widely and lit up. My mam rented out video films from one of her shops in the Page Moss district of Liverpool, and these videos were the pornographic films that I had jokingly asked her to send from her shop, so the lads would be entertained. I knew the lads would be happy with these videos when the chance came for them to be played. The other parcel was from my dad. I jokingly thought that it must have hurt his wallet to send me this parcel. There were a few bars of chocolate and a few other useful things in it, such as packets of wet wipes that would help me to freshen up when there wouldn't be a chance to wash properly. In addition, there were a few bars of soap. I hoped my dad would have sent me some pornographic magazines to go with the films that my mam had sent me, but no such luck. I wrote back to them and thanked them for the parcels. A letter came from Paula, and I was extremely happy to hear from her. Paula sent me a birthday card to send to my half-brother, Ian, as it was his birthday in a couple of weeks. I wrote the card out with heart-felt words to my half-brother, and, then, I wrote to Paula as well. There were times when I wrote to Paula a couple of times a day.

Jay received a load of letters from pen pigs. Once Jay finished scrutinising his mail, he turned round to me and said, "Are you going to stick the porn on Scouse?"

"Fucking too right," I said enthusiastically.

The admin tent was the fullest I've seen in a long time because the good news about the porn films travelled fast around here. As I placed one of the porn films in the video player and pressed play, I turned round to see the expressions on all the lad's faces as the film came on. Their eyes, peering straight forward, were nearly popping out of their sockets and theirs mouths were wide open, for they haven't seen anything like this since we'd been over here. Seemingly, it appeared that they never saw a naked woman's body before. A big loud cheer erupted from inside the tent as a huge pair of breasts filled the tele screen. A few lads left half way through the film and returned back five minutes later a bit flushed and reddened in the face. I reckon that they snuck off to the toilet for a quick wank. I could picture a queue of lads, who waited outside the toilet to pull the heads off their dicks. Jay found out that there would be a phone run on tomorrow, and I couldn't wait to speak to Paula.

I was able to get myself on the phone run to Camp 4 this morning. It was a bit different when we went in the morning because the phone cards didn't last as long as they did at night. We arrived at Camp 4 about nine-thirty in the morning and with the time difference of three hours, I waited till 10:30am to call her. Paula would just be getting up and ready for work. Therefore, I passed the time away in the camp's burger bar. Their burger bar was no McDonalds; instead, it was more like a trucker's café. I bought myself a dodgy looking cheeseburger for my breakfast. They weren't that nice, but they did the trick. After I finished my burger, I went to look for a phone that actually worked. I had a good chance of one phone being free in the early time of day. I put the handset to my left ear and pushed the digits with a pen, dialling her phone number. It rang three times before the call was answered. It wasn't Paula that picked the phone up; it was her mother.

"Is Paula there please?" I asked her mother politely.

"No." Paula's mother retorted nastily.

"Has she already left for work?" I asked her.

"She doesn't live here any more! Thanks to you," she shouted at me.

Then, she slammed the phone down. I was shocked and still had the phone held to my ear. The bad news took a few seconds to sink in. I didn't know what to do, for I hadn't received a bluey from Paula that said there was trouble back home. My head was choker with confusion has my chin dropped down to my chest. There wasn't much more I could do till a bit later when I could phone Paula's work up and talk with her.

Meanwhile, I waited till I could phone Paula at work. Time was languid and lifeless in-between the time I talked to Paula's mother till I was actually able to talk with Paula. When the time came, I phoned Paula's work up, but Paula didn't answer; instead, another girl answered, "Is Paula there, please?" I asked her.

"No, she isn't here today. It's her day off," the other girl informed me.

By this point, I was worried especially since I couldn't track Paula down. I decided to phone my mum up at her Page Moss shop to see if she knew of anything about the whereabouts of Paula. Shelly, my mum's assistant, answered the phone, "Is me mam there, Shelly?" I asked her worried and anxiously.

"No," she replied.

"Yeah don't know where Paula is do yeah?" I asked Shelly.

"Yeah, I do. Paula's wrote yeah a letter with her new address and to let yeah know what's gone on," Shelly informed me.

"Cheers, Shell. I'll see yeah later ta-ra," I sighed with relief as I placed the hand set back on the receiver.

I couldn't stop thinking where Paula could be, as we headed back to our location. I didn't need this shit while I was over here. I got enough to worry about like the Iraqi's and any other unexpected happenings of being in a war. When we returned to our location the mail had come in, and there were a few bluey's that waited for me. None of the bluey's were from Paula, but instead from a couple of mates from back home telling me about their nights out on the piss and going to raves.

I managed to get myself settled down to write a few bluey's. My head was still battered with the wonder of where Paula had gone. Therefore, I decided to write to Paula's parents. And in my letter, I asked why it was my fault that she wasn't living there anymore. I explained that it had nothing to do with me, and that I was over here in the desert getting ready to fight a war, so I couldn't have anything to do with why she left. I couldn't do anything right in their eyes because we didn't get on with each other, and that upset Paula. Also, I wrote to Paula in care of my mam's address to find out what had happened.

25

When I woke up this morning, I was still on a downer. No mail had come in for me today, which made matters even worse in my head. Nevertheless, I thought I might have gotten a letter from Paula to explain what on earth happened back home. A few of the other lads took the piss out of me when I told them what had happened with Paula's mam on the phone, saying that Paula had another bloke. I pondered on the idea, but I knew Paula wasn't that type of girl. All I knew was that I didn't need this shit under the present circumstances. I thought it would be great, if I had the bottle just to walk into the middle of the desert and blow my brains out of the back of my skull. Depression started to set in quickly.

I went into Node Command and had a word with Lieutenant Naden, "It's not just the events that are happening back home, but out here as well, sir. I want to be somewhere were I can do me trade," I told him with a saddened and sorrowful look.

Lieutenant Naden seemed to know how I felt. I've been feeling pissed off for a bit with not doing any radio operating and just getting dicked to do all the shit jobs.

"Next time there is a phone run on, I'll make sure you get to go," Lieutenant Naden said in a concerning voice.

He also told me that we would be moving location soon.

I hated it here in this Trunk Node now. I'd rather get to a brigade, where I could crack on with operating some sets. So, I went back to my tent where it was empty, and started to pack my Bergen with all my kit, and even folded up my camp cot and placed it across the top of the Bergen. My mind was so confused, and all I wanted to do was leave this location and get to a brigade. My Bergen was heavy, and I struggled placing the straps over my shoulders. I decided that I wasn't going to take my 1-Tonnie; instead, I was going to walk down to the MSR and hitch a lift north towards to the front line and a brigade. There was nobody about as I sneaked out of my tent and climbed over the little hill of crushed stones beside my tent. I didn't get very far; I didn't even get out of the stone quarry because my Bergen was too heavy to walk with. I thought I would get arrested and charged with desertion, even though my intention was to head north closer to the fighting. I turned back and sneaked back into my tent the same way I left. Nobody noticed that I was missing, so on my return to my tent I set up my camp cot again and unpacked my Bergen. When I went to bed, I laid back and everything just spun around in my head. I didn't think a move to a new location would change anything.

Waking up the next morning, I felt a lot better. The sun's rays were beating down upon my face through the flaps of the tent. Seemingly, it was going to be a wonderful day, so I gave myself a good wash and a shower. Because we were going to be on the move shortly, I thought I should crack on with working on my 1-Tonnie and my radio equipment. I emptied my mast boxes out, gave the pegs a clean and tidied the guy ropes. The sets were so dusty that I gave them a wipe down and checked the batteries in them. Once I was finished with my vehicle, I trotted over to give a few of the lads a hand lifting the SPAM generator onto the back of the POL wagon. We were told by Staff Large that the generator would be exchanged for kit with the SPAMs, and I knew us junior ranks wouldn't see any of it. Only the senior ranks saw the kit.

One of the Sergeants came over to me and let me know that I was on the phone run this afternoon. I was very made up now, for maybe I could find out what happened back home. There were six of us going, Jay, Tiny, Jim, Gaz, Rick and I, all rode in the back of the Land Rover on our way to Camp 4 to make our phone calls. We laughed uncontrollably the whole way there, as we took the piss out of the seniors in our troop as we usually did; plus, it cheered us all up, although it didn't take much to raise our morale of late. Since it was the afternoon, I phoned Paula up at work trying to get a hold of her. I couldn't get through because the line was engaged. I decided to risk the balance of my stomach, and I went to get myself a cheeseburger from the camp burger bar. The burger was made from the strangest beef I'd ever tasted; in fact, I'm sure it was camel meat. After eating my burger, I strolled casually back to the phones, hoping this time the line wouldn't be busy. When I dialed, I successfully got through. The phone rang and Paula answered. I was over the moon with joy when I heard her voice, for I finally reached her. This phone call made up for all the blueys that I hadn't received from her over the past few days.

"Sorry I haven't wrote to you for a while, Pete. I've been dead busy moving into my new flat. My mum kicked me out of the house because I'm still seeing you. The flat is costing me one hundred and fifty pounds a month," she told me.

"I'll tell yeah what, go and live in me mam's because I don't want yeah living in a flat on yeah own. Look, I have to go now because the pips are going. I'll write a bluey to me mam, love yeah." I slowly replaced the hand set back on the receiver.

I couldn't believe what had gone on. Nevertheless, I felt much better now that I knew Paula was all right.

On our way back to our location, a few of us were complaining that since we were ordered to retake our NAPS tablets again, we were feeling the symptoms of being lethargic all the time and also suffered from the reoccurring headaches. It seemed too much of a coincidence that we had these symptoms only when we took the NAPS tablets. None of us would dare to report sick with our symptoms because we knew that we wouldn't be taken seriously and could even be accused of trying to avoid going to war.

When we arrived back at our location we were informed that we were moving location later on that day and that the Node would be moving up north to 7 Brigade's location. This was our war starting; at last, it gave us all a little bit of a high esteem, knowing that we were on the move away from this location never to return. We sat at this location since New Years Day, five weeks was way too long to sit in one location. Jay, Jim and I got stuck in right away with packing away our personnel kit. Once we had placed our kit in our respective vehicles, we cracked on and dismantled our 9ft x 9ft tent. It was a bit of a nightmare, getting it out from beneath all the sand, which had changed into mud in the recent rainstorms. Once the kit was packed away, we helped the slop jockeys and Staff Large to dismantle the admin tent. Sergeant Clay built a little bonfire in the corner of our location to burn all the rubbish we didn't need to take with us. It took the entire troop to hurriedly pack up the Node and line up all the wagons in convoy in just under an hour. We must have all been very keen on leaving this place. Once Staff Large made sure we hadn't left anything behind, we made our way out of the quarry and headed north along the MSR even closer to the Saudi Arabian border with Iraq.

The journey north, along the MSR bored the others and me as well. I'd been most of this way before when I needed to pick up the other Relay dets with Lieutenant Naden and dropped them off at other Nodes. I had Jim and little Dave travelling in my 1-Tonnie with me. Dave was a Relay Op on Gaz Tuff's det with Tiny. It would have been very cramped in the cab of the Relay wagon if all three of them traveled together, so to make it more comfortable in the cab Dave traveled in the back of my 1-Tonnie. Dave just took the knock after about twenty minutes. I couldn't believe this lad, and he could fall asleep on a washing line. After about two hours of driving, we stopped off at a troggy shop on the MSR. It wasn't worth us stopping off at all, for there was nothing on the shelves in the way of anything edible. I managed to get myself a couple of cans of cold Pepsi Cola. We were informed by Staff Large that this would be our last resting point until we reached our new location, so if anyone wanted to have a piss that this was their last chance. After we had emptied our bladder the word came round for us all to mount our wagons and ready ourselves to move off. I jumped into Tiny's wagon, and Gaz jumped into mine to drive. I was very tired, and I didn't want to risk having a smash or falling asleep behind the wheel of a very expensive, but unsophisticated built vehicle. We pulled out onto the MSR, still heading north. I didn't know how long it would be before we went deep into the desert. The only thing I did know for sure was that it would be dark when we arrived there.

When we arrived in our new location, it was pitch black, and I didn't know what time it was because I didn't wear a watch. I knew we had travelled for about nine hours, and we were all absolutely drained of energy. The days that we drove for hours on end took all the energy and vigour out of us. When all the wagons were put in their positions, Staff Large grabbed everyone to empty out the admin wagon, so he and Sergeant Clay could get to their beds. What a cheek they had. They could have slept under the stars like the rest of us lads. It really pissed us off, for we weren't sure if it was late or early, whichever way we wanted to look at it, these pair of selfish twats looked after themselves. We finally unloaded the wagon, so the lads grabbed their doss bags and made their beds on the desert floor under the stars. I managed to squeeze into the small cavity in the back of my 1-Tonnie. The Jack attitude amongst the seniors wasn't just restricted to our Node, but the lads from other Nodes had said the same about their senior ranks when we had met up with them. I wondered if it was like this throughout the whole Royal Signals.

Just has the sun broke over the desert horizon, everyone was up, out of their pits and were getting our new location into some sort of order. When the new location was nearly completed, an order came round for us to pack up and be ready to move by 10:00a.m. Everyone ran round like blue arse flies and tore all the tents down that we had just sweated our bollocks off to erect. I began to have a SHF (*sense of humour failure*)

Saudi Arabian sunset at our third location.

with this 'on the bus off the bus' behaviour, moving from place to place without knowing when we would go and where we would be going. The British Army is renowned amongst its troops for always doing that sort of thing. The whole Node was packed and lined up ready to move by 9:45a.m. And by 11:00a.m, there was still no notice to move.

"Fuck this for a game of soldiers. I'm off to catch some UV's," I told Jay.

I climbed up on top of my wagon, took my top off and laid down on my back soaking up the hot desert sun. It felt nice in the morning as the sun beat down on my naked torso. Although teatime came quickly and there was still no notice to move out. Staff Large told Hutch to rustle up a little something for everyone in the Node. After tea, I went straight for my bed to have an early night's sleep, just in case we got the nod to move out at silly o'clock in the morning.

26

Sergeant Clay came round, roused us all awake and told us to prepare to move. The time was a very early 1:00a.m. Just as I thought, silly o'clock in the morning, and, then, we moved away at 2:00a.m. My mind kicked into combat mode. I didn't have a clue as to where we were going neither did Gaz, who travelled with me in the 1-Tonnie. After a few hours of driving, I started to feel a bit unwell, so Gaz took over and drove. I didn't know what was wrong with me. I thought I was starting to come down with a twenty-four hour bug or something related to the NAPS tablets I had religiously been taking since being reordered to take them. I tried to get some shuteye, but it was useless. As we drove night soon became day and the sun made it another glorious day. As we approached our destination there were all the other Nodes from our squadron and other squadrons lined up in packets (*rows of vehicles*). Our Node pulled up along side Node 043, and we formed our own packet.

When we pulled up and went down to see Danny Steele, who was a technical store man with 043. I knew Danny from when I joined the junior army after I left school in 1987. Danny and I were in Kohima Troop together. We had been in contact occasionally with each other because I still wrote to his sister, Sonia, when I left the juniors. I asked him if he had heard from his sister or his mam. He didn't really get on with his sister, but he had just received a food parcel from his mam the other day. There was a letter in the parcel he told me telling that Sonia was pregnant with her first child. This news came as a shock to me as Sonia was a couple of years younger than me. I asked Danny for his mam's address, which he gave me, so I could write a bluey to Sonia to see how she was getting on and to wish her all the best. Once I had his mam's address he gave me a bowl of Sugar Puffs for my breakfast. I dug my camera out to take a few pictures of the lads and a Warrior Tracked Armoured Vehicle, which was the transport of the British infantry. The word came round for us to get into NBC stage 2 again, which meant we put on our NBC suites, boots and gloves. We sat round for about thirty minutes before we started our engines and moved off in convoy formation.

I was feeling a lot better after the Sugar Puffs, so I drove and it was about thirty to forty-five minutes before our Node came to a stand still.

Lining up to practice our invasion of Iraq.

When we pulled up, I couldn't believe my eyes. I'd never saw anything like it before, not even in a war film. There were all kinds of military vehicles for as far as the eye could see. There were hundreds possibly thousands, ranging from Challenger Main Battle Tanks to motorbikes. Even a few Westland Lynx and Gazelle helicopters flew closely and loudly over our heads. It was an awesome sight that gave me a good natural buzz and proud to be British. We had learnt from our seniors that this was a practice run for when we would cross the breach into Iraq. In the army, every formation from an infantry section to a divisional battle group always rehearsed how they would engage the enemy in battle before doing it for real. While we sat round and waited for the order to move, we heard a rumour that a lad from the Artillery had just shot himself. We didn't know how true this information was, and it may have been just a Chinese whisper that got out of control. The next bit of information that came round was that he was dead, and that the bullet went through his throat and out the other side of the nape of his neck. I thought that he mustn't have been able to handle the pressure.

There's no way I would consider killing myself after coming this far. I know I wouldn't have the balls to do it like the other month when I wanted to do it. Sergeant Clay came round to all the wagons and told us to start our engines. Our packet moved off five minutes later. I drove along a track that had already been made by other wheeled vehicles. There was another track to my left that was only being used by tracked vehicles such as tanks and artillery howitzer guns. We drove round in a huge circle for about twenty minutes before our packet stopped again.

Staff Large came round with the MREs that I gave to the slop jockeys for everyone and told us that we would be here for some time. The reason Staff Large gave us the MREs to eat was because it wouldn't be worth setting up the cookers to do us a cooked meal, as we didn't know how long we would be here. The MRE that I was given was one of the nice ones. They didn't have the type of meal written on the outer wrapper, so it's a lucky dip on which meal you got. I had the meatballs in barbecue sauce, and it was scrumpish. To polish it off, I ate the cheese spread on the cream crackers. We prayed that we had cheese spread and crackers in the MRE because it was better than the actual meal half the time. Once I had finished eating, my body was telling me to go on a shovel recce.

I grabbed my shovel and looked across the desert to find a likely spot to empty the undigested parts of my meal. There was no tree or bush in the desert that I could hide behind and keep my dignity intact. However, I did notice a small mound of sand to my left, which would have to do. I needed to get there quickly in time because my bodily waste started to touch my boxer shorts. I shuffled over there, clenching tight both my arse cheeks to keep it all in. The worse thing about this situation was the fact that I was still in my NBC suit. As I got closer to the mound of sand, it became clear to me that it was a tank trench. This would be a lot better, has I would be able to do my business in peace and away from any glaring eyes.

The trench was about thirty feet long with a gradual slope that led down into a giant hole made for the tanks. Obviously, this trench had once been the home of a large tracked vehicle like a tank. I dug a little hole with my shovel, lent against the wall of the trench and squatted over the little hole. I lifted the back of my NBC suit up with my left hand and pulled the straps from my trousers round to the front with my right hand, so I would not shit and piss all over them. No sooner than my trousers were down round my ankles, my arse hole opened, and I moved my bowels loudly and with a vowel stench. It was long, hard, and it was a relief to get it out. I seemingly resembled a Japanese sniper by the way I squinted and frowned. I reached for the roll of comfy bum toilet paper and cleaned my arse really well. I back filled the hole that I dug and made sure I totally covered all bodily waste, and, when I returned to my wagon, I dug the wet wipes out of my Bergen, which my dad sent me to clean my hands.

By the way things looked that particular day we would be spending the night at this location, sleeping in our wagons.

"Staff Large can go to fuck if he thinks I'm unloading his Bedford so he can get a good night's kip," I told Jay.

Jay nodded his head in agreement.

Early in the morning, it was silly o'clock again when we were woken up and readied to move off. A Military Policeman came down to our packet and told us to follow the artillery wagons. There was something amiss with the artillery wagons in front, but I could only see a few of their convoy lights. I visually managed to calculate five wagons. Sergeant Clay stopped our convoy and came down to tell us that the artillery was lost; in addition, they lost half of their own unit. At this point, we parted company with the gunners, and we made our own way to our next location. Our unit travelled so far from where we were that time had gone from night to day again by the time we reached our new location. This new location looked quite familiar, and, then, it dawned on me; we were here just the other day. I could see for miles and miles in all different directions. The desert floor was as flat as a pancake. All the wagons were placed into their positions, and everyone hurriedly spent no time in setting up our location. We got faster and faster at setting up our location every time.

I noticed a Bedford in the distance, which was heading directly towards our location. This Bedford was a Relay wagon. I was actually able to see the people who were inside the cab. There was Flinnie, Wilkie and Gaz Eastlake drove the wagon. Flinnie flung his head out of the window and loudly shouted to me, "I've got some home brew in the back. Come round to our tent tonight for a drink, Scouse."

They were returning after being attached to another Node for a week and I hadn't realised they had left our Node.

I thought my home brew should be ready now too, for it had fermented a fortnight. There wasn't much daylight left, and I needed to get out of my filthy combats and have a good bollock wash. I felt so clean and refreshed afterwards. There was even a bit of time to wash all my dirty clothes. I draped the clothes all over the cam-nets to dry out. Even though there wasn't much daylight left I knew it would still be warm enough for my clothes dry. Afterwards, Jay and I went over to Flinnie's tent for a game of cards and a drink. I took along some of my own poison to help the night go on with a bang.

27

My brew was ready, and so was I and the rest of the lads, and along with Flinnie's brew, we were going to have a hell of a time getting pissed like back home in the pubs. When we got inside Flinnie's tent and settled down, Flinnie placed some plastic cups on top of the drink cooler, and I filled them up for the four of us. I swore that the cups started to melt with the strength of the ale. The brewed ale was cream in colour and had a very strong taste, such as Vodka. When I took a mouthfull, my eyes almost popped out of their sockets the ale was so strong. And I felt a burning sensation in the back of my throat as it made its way down to my stomach. It was quite excellent and would get us well pissed. I poured my batch of ale into the drink cooler and mixed it with Flinnie's, and the brew turned out to be one lethal tonic, although it wasn't long before I started to feel the effects of being boozily tipsy. We never got to drink out here with Saudi being an Islamic country and it was against their laws to drink alcohol. I enjoyed the drink and the feeling of being drunk made my head light and took all the feelings and thoughts out of my head of being out here in the desert about to fight a war, and the thoughts I'd been having of being away from Paula and home. I seemingly didn't have a care in the world that night; indeed, it was regeneratively sound. All of a sudden the tent flaps swiftly parted, and Warbie poked his head in and said, "Come on Scouse. You're on stag with me now," he informed me.

Warbie was a Relay Op from Wigan in Lancashire, which is at the other end of the M58 from Liverpool. He was a sound lad, so I stuffed a drink in his hand before we done our one-hour stag, and said, "Here, Warbie, have a drink first, and, then, we'll go stag on."

I wasn't in the mood to do this prowl stag, for I had drunk a bit too much, but I had to do my job under any circumstances, and I did. As I stood up to leave, I staggered out of the tent leaning sideways when I walked, but I made it, for being a squaddie, I was used to being pissed quite a lot; however, I nearly fell flat on my face when I left the confines of Flinnie's dwarfish tent. The evening air smacked me right in the face and was refreshing, "I don't think I'm going to make this next hour, Warbie," I slurred to him with the odd hick-ups in-between words.

Warbie burst into fits of laughter, has I staggered around our location and tripped over some of the tents guy ropes when we both went to check on the slop jockey's tent. This seemed too much for me because I drank so much, but I managed to persuade Warbie to go back to Flinnie's tent for a skive, and another drink. I didn't think he would approve by the deepened frowned expression on his face. But, we stayed at Flinnie's for a quick one before having another prowl about the desert night. That stag was the quickest hour's stag that I'd ever completed. As soon as we were relieved from stag, I headed straight back to Flinnie's tent to carry on with the drinking session. I loved tonight's drink. I invited Warbie back for another drink, but he declined my offer.

When I rejoined our little party, the lads were in the middle of a card game and there was still plenty of ale left, but because I was a drunken menace, they wouldn't let me join in the card game. As that night grew later and later, my eyes got heavier and heavier. So, I mumbled to the lads, "I'll think I'll write a bluey to Paula since yeah won't let me join in the game. Yeah gang of arlarses."

Then, Jay, Flinnie and Wilkie began to burst out in fits of laughter because I was so pissing drunk and slurring my words. Therefore, I grabbed a bluey and wrote to Paula, but I was so pissed that I didn't even know what I wrote; thus, I wondered if she would understand what I wrote, whenever she received and read the letter.

I couldn't even remember how I managed the short walk from Flinnie's tent to my tent on my own. In fact, I slightly remember that Jay and Flinnie both had a hold of me underneath each of my arms practically holding me up as they dragged me with my feet trailing in the sand leaving two parallel tracks behind, "Hey lads, I think it's time for a singsong," I told them.

And, then, I burst out the chorus of, 'In my Liverpool Home', singing, "In my Liverpool home, we speak with an accent exceedingly rare, we meet under a statue extremely bare. And if yeah want a cathedral, we've got one to spare. In my Liverpool home, where? In my Liverpool, tralie la," I tried to sing.

Surprisingly, I didn't startle awake the whole Node while I loudly bawled the songs out into night.

I suddenly felt the urge to go to the toilet.

"Lads, I need a burst. You'll have to stop," I told them.

I couldn't stand up on my own nor could I remember unzipping my combats and getting my dick out to relieve myself. The only explanation could be that one of the lads must have been a real good mate and got my dick out for me, pointed it in a safe direction, shook it and placed it back. After that, they continued to carry me to my tent and threw me down like a dead weight on my camp cot. As I laid on my cot, Jim was still up reading a book, and I burst into singsongs again. As I laid there and sung totally out of tune, I felt the tent start to go round and round, spinning real fast in all different directions too. The inside of the tent became intensely blurred to me, and I felt the urge to be sick. But, I couldn't move my body, so I turned my head to my right and let it dangle down over the edge of my camp cot. Jim's webbing was directly below me and in the way.

"Jim, Jim, move yeah webbing!" I shouted at him.

"Why should I do that, Scouse?" he asked.

"Because I'm going to be sick all over it if you don't shift it," I muttered to him.

I never saw anyone reach for their kit so fast in my entire army career. He dived straight off his camp cot as quick as he thought about it, grabbed his webbing by the yoke and dragged it away just as my vomit splattered into the sand below, spraying about the tent. My head dangled over the edge of my camp cot with my eyes lids half opened, my eyes rolled back in my head and vomit dripping off of my chin. Coming round and wiping the pieces of puke off of my chin with the back of my hand, I felt much better, falling into a deep intoxicated sleep, and I slept soundly until the next morning when I awoke feeling like death warmed up. Moans and groans of being hung-over came from my part of the tent although my head started not to feel all that bad the more I woke up, considering how much I drank the night before. The tent stunk with an awful sickly smell, so I grabbed a handful of sand and covered the stale vomit that lay next to my cot. The few lads that seen the state I was in the previous night took the piss out of me, which I thought they'd been planning from seeing me the night before. This sparingly and consequential misery of behaviour lasted for most of the morning, and then, diligently back to work I went.

I got to grips with tidying out the back of my 1-Tonnie, with all the travelling we'd done over the past few days, and Sergeant Clay, Jim and I went on a VHF comms exercise for the afternoon to check the range of the antennas to see how far away we could work. We started off with a two-meter whip antenna whilst we were mobile until we lost comms after quite a few miles, which Sergeant Clay logged in his notebook. When the vehicle became static, I threw an extra one-metre section of antenna on to make it into three-metres. The exercise was a bit shit, but it made a change to actually get some hands on, on the sets, concentrating most of the day with the sets. After this actual workday was over, Jay, Jim and I spent the evening together and caught up on our mail. I wrote a bluey to Sonia, Danny Steele's sister, wishing her all the best with the baby. It had been at least a couple of years since I last wrote or even spoke to Sonia. I suggested to her in the bluey that if she were to have a baby boy that she should name him Peter, after her favourite Scouser, me. Sonia didn't know I was head over heals in love and was planning on getting married the following year, so I wrote my good news to her. I also asked her to pass on my regards to her mam. We thought the people back home must have gotten worried, for they hadn't heard from us for a few days. Nonetheless, the next day would arrive soon, so I took the bluey's to the post box before getting very much needed sleep.

Today was the 8th of February 1991. It was Ian's, my half brother's, ninth birthday. He lived with my mam and her husband, the man she had the affair with when I was younger, in their terraced house in Anfield, Liverpool. I wrote to Ian, wishing him a happy birthday and letting him know what I'd been up to for the past few days.

28

Right after I wrote to Ian, Sergeant Clay came into our tent and ordered Jim and me to go to OSC (*Operational System Control*) 135's location for a briefing on tomorrow's comms exercise. Jim and I didn't have a clue, as to what OSC was with only being new into the army, but we had an idea that it was to do with comms. As I climbed inside my 1-Tonnie, Staff Large came over and started to give me shit over the cam net not covering both Land Rovers. "If yeah didn't keep on dicking us for these stupid dick jobs all the time, the cam-net would have been sorted," I snarled at him with a mean leer before driving over to OSC's location.

Staff Large didn't say anything back to me because he knew I was in the right. At the briefing with OSC, we were given the timings for when the exercise was to start, along with the frequencies that included the lost comms procedure in the CEI (*Communications Electronic Instructions*). The briefing at OSC 135 didn't last that long and, shortly afterwards, we started to head back to our own location. At our location, Jim and I cracked on sorting out our cam-net to keep Staff Large off of our backs for a bit. We finished sorting the cam-net just in time for mail call.

The mail sacks got emptied out quickly, but not a one letter was for me. I hadn't received any letters or parcels from Paula, my mother or my dad for about five days. A few of the lads had already started to receive Valentine cards from their wives, girlfriends or mistresses, for some of the guys got mail from both their wives and girlfriends. Once again, my morale took a large swirling depressive nosedive, for it's been a while since I received any mail, and my mental state was a bit traumatized, affecting my attitude, emotions, and my mind simply wasn't right. However, that night, most of the other guys read over their cards and other post. I was feeling so down that after our tea, I went back to my tent and just sulked. I wrote yet again to Paula letting her know that I had not received any bluey's from her lately. After placing the bluey in the postbox I decided to call it quits for the day and decided to have an early night.

The next day, Sergeant Clay, Jim and I went on the comms exercise. I'd done most of the radio operating whilst Jim drove. Sergeant Clay was in his vehicle reading the map. Today's exercise was mainly a voice procedure to test everyone's capability with the sets. This exercise lasted for a few hours until the officers back at OSC were happy enough to call 'end ex' (*end of exercise*). This was the first real chance I'd gotten to use a set since I finished trade training last July. I was a Rad Op, but didn't do anything but mess round since we arrived in the desert. I wanted to do what I was trained to do, operate the sets, sending and receiving messages. I worked in a Node, which were full Ptarmigan equipment and the gear of the Relay Ops to operate the equipment. The problem with a Node from a Rad Ops perspective was it spent most of its time static. Therefore, there was no need for Rad Ops until the Node was on the move. Jim and I were mildly ill tempered and bothersome over this situation because we couldn't do what we were trained to do, that's all we wanted to do, and, therefore, most of the time we spent idling back at our location writing bluey's and doing Staff Large's dick jobs. I knew tonight was the 'Merseyside Derby' between the Everton and Liverpool Football Clubs and I mentioned this in a bluey that I wrote to my mate, Mick, and I also wrote that I would try and listen to it live on a radio.

I didn't have a short wave radio, which we were recommended to bring with us; instead, I tuned in the 321 Clansman HF set that was mounted in the back of my 1-Tonnie to BBC (*British Broadcasting Corporation*) World Service and listened to the Football match on that radio channel. I was able to do this because the BBC broadcasted the derby in HF, or in civvie terms, AM band. Whilst I was listening to the game, I wrote to Howard Kendal, the manager of Everton Football Club, to see if the club would be nice enough to send one of their supporters, risking his life for Queen and country a couple of freebies. One of the lads, from our Node, got a personnel letter from Greame Souness, the Glasgow Rangers Football Club's manager, along with a couple of club badges and autographs from the first team. I hoped Everton would be as generous as Rangers and send something to me. When the match finished, I shouted out intensely, "Fucking redneck bastards," for Liverpool won the match by three goals to Everton's one.

Because of the loss, when I left my 1-Tonnie I stayed in my tent for the rest of the night. Even though I come from Liverpool, I have always supported Everton Football Club as it is traditional that a son follows in his father's footsteps and supports the same football team as his father. I knew the rest of the lads listened to the match, but I just couldn't face the stick that they would give me. And, soon, my turn came round to go on stag duty.

The time was midnight, and I stagged on with Rick Sheriff who was the Nodes storeman. The night dragged by in-between 12:00am and 2:00a.m. During stag duty, the surrounding areas were nearly pitch black and deadly silent. The highlight of the stag was seeing all the missiles impetuously dropping down out of the sky up Northward from our location. Afar in the clear night sky, we saw tiny green lights that heavily fell and dropping to the Earth, blinding small areas where the bright shining stars, illuminating the sky and allotting the sights of the countless planes flying all about. We presumed they were missiles because further on the horizon the sky turned a lighter shade of blue, which only lasted for a second or two. Therefore, the tiny green lights had to have been definitely missiles, for we knew that both the American and British Air Forces were on the offence, dropping bombs, attacking the Iraqi's, subliming their defensive positions for hours upon hours unstopping. Consequently, on the other side, the Iraqis were on the defence, firing anti-aircraft weaponry at the allied planes that carried numerous and various types of bombs of their own far above in the night sky and firing Scud missiles at Israel and Saudi. We just sat there and watched as the Iraqis tried but failed against the combined strength of the allied forces. And by the time the attack finished, Rick Harvey and Cocksie came to relieve us from stag duty, so we could get some sleep. They had the graveyard stag from 2:00am till 4:00am.

The first thing I'd done this morning was switch on my sets to check how much power was left in the batteries. There wasn't much charge left in the cells at all, so, I disconnected the batteries from the sets and connected them to my generator to place them on the charge. I thought I needed a new set of batteries; however, the batteries were much further down on the bottom of the pecking order for the replacement parts. Then, I watched as Lieutenant Naden walked straight towards us. Lieutenant Naden came over to tell me that Jim and I were going along to OSC 135 with him for a brief on another comms exercise. Once we were there, the YoS (*Yeoman of Signals*) informed us that all of the Node's Rad Ops would be working together in a joint HF and VHF exercise. The OSC was call sign zero, and the radio detachments started with us, being one-zero.

The VHF comms worked in a range of about thirty kilometers with a three-meter whip antenna, and the HF worked in a range of about twenty kilometers on a four-meter whip, which we found out the other day on the other comms exercise. Also, we tested our Elevated VHF antenna. The 'EVHF' antenna was much more powerful than a normal whip antenna, more infrangibly sturdy and high-tech, and we could only use this antenna in a static location because the antenna needed to be erected high on top of a mast. In the British Army, we nicknamed the 'EVHF,' a 'Pineapple,' for all of the pieces of metal on it. We screwed a 3.75-metre whip to the top of the Pineapple and a coaxial cable plugged right into it. The other end of the coaxial cable went plugged straight into the front of a Clansman 353 VHF set to complete the erected antenna. Once I tuned into the frequency that I needed to be on, I gave OSC a radio check.

"Hello. Zero, this is one-zero. Radio check, over," I spoke directly into the handset that was connected to the radio.

"Zero, okay, over,"

The radio reply came back quickly and clearly from OSC.

"One-zero. Okay, out," I concluded.

Whilst Jim packed up the equipment, I noticed that we parked nearly right next to a desert rat's hole. The desert rat kept on poking its head out and looking round. One time, when I managed to get my camera out in time, I took a picture of the desert rat when it poked its head out of the hole once again. End Ex was called, and we didn't spare the horses to get back to our location. We rushed back to see if we got any letters or parcels. And, I did.

Mail call was early today, and I received three bluey's from Paula, one from my mam and one from Mickey Doyle, the latter being a Sergeant in the '1st Battalion Irish Guards.' He was Irish Guards current recruitment Sergeant at Liverpool's army career's office. I got to know Mickey a few months ago from my fortnight stint in Liverpool as a 'Satisfied Soldier' before I went on my posting to Germany. In Mickey's letter, he told me that people back home brought all kinds of parcels into the career's office to be sent to squaddies in the Gulf. Mickey put my name and address on a few of them before they got sent out. Also, Mickey said that there were a few loony lefty students in Liverpool city center, who called out for the removal of British forces from Saudi Arabia. I thought the cheek of them, for they never got themselves a job to stop sponging off of us taxpayers; moreover, I vaguely believed that half of them were not even from Britain. With rapidity, I replied back to all of my mail before I needed to get my 1-Tonnie ready for another exercise.

I hadn't been told the details about this exercise; only that it involves the whole Node except for the slop jockeys. One of the Techs, Sam, travelled with me in the 1-Tonnie for the exercise. This exercise wasn't a comms exercise, but it was more of a movement exercise. I wouldn't need the vehicles' sets, so I kept the HF set tuned into BBC World Service. During the exercise, we just drove round in a big circle stopping and starting all the time. I must admit the exercise beat sitting in our location and getting dicked for silly no-nonsense jobs again. One of the places that we stopped at was in the middle of a SPAM tank unit's location. The word came down the line from Staff Large that we would be stopping here for at least an hour.

All of the tanks were desert camouflaged painted with a sandy brown paint. The SPAM tank unit was part of the American's 1st Armoured Division, 'The Big Red One.' Years ago, I watched a film that starred the famous actor, Lee Marvin, about this division, and how they took their name and badge from a German unit in World War I. I left my 1-Tonnie and went over to one of the SPAM tanks, which were called M1A1 Abraham main battle tank. The Abraham tanks were equivalent to our British Challenger 1 main battle tank. One of the SPAMs allowed me to go inside the turret, and I had a look round. Inside the tank was quite spacious, and they had a four-man crew. This was very exciting for me because I'd never been inside a tank before, let alone one that belonged to another country, and that seemed oddly funny to me, putting a slight grin on my face. After seeing where the ammunition was stored, the driver's seat, the gunners position as well as the tank commanders position, and after a good informed look around the inside I climbed back out of the turret to pay attention to the outside of the Abraham. On the tank's barrel was sprayed in thick jet-black paint, 'No Name.' Every one of the SPAM unit's tanks had been given a nickname by their crewmembers, and all the writings were sprayed in thick jet-black paint on the barrel. I asked one of the crewmembers, "Why did you write 'No name' for a name on your tank?"

A whimsical SPAM replied, "Our crew couldn't think of a good name for our tank. And while we were thinking of a name, we weren't able to come up with any name good enough. Then, one of our crewmembers said,

"We don't have no name for our tank. That's great. Now, we're the only ones with no name."

Then, I cut in and said, "That's a good name; 'No Name.' Let's name

American M1A1 Main Battle Tank 'No Name'.

our tank 'No Name.' And, that's how we came up with the name. And right off, we sprayed it on the barrel of the tank."

Nicely, I gave one of the SPAMs my Royal Signals cap badge as a souvenir, and I explained to the SPAM that the cap badge was a figure of Mercury, messenger of the Greek Gods. He became all made up with it, and, in return, he gave me a 'Big Red One' combat shoulder badge. The badge was green with a black number one in the middle of it, and it was in the shape of a shield. Furthermore, he gave me a bandoleer of 7.62-mm rounds from his M60 machine gun. It was a fair swap, I thought. The SPAM told me that they had plenty of rounds, and that they wouldn't miss a load. I took the bandoleer, and I put it across my chest, making me look like Rambo.

I took the SPAM over to have a look at my wagon. There was a bit of a difference between his tank and my 1-Ton Land Rover. Obviously, he was just as impressed with my 'battle bus' as I was with his tank. I could tell from the awed look, dropped draw and raised brows on his face. And then, he asked me if I would swap one of the vehicles registration plates for his American Army issue CBA (*combat body armour*). We hadn't been issued with any body armour yet, so I went up on the roof of my wagon with a screwdriver to prise it off when he realized that he might be in need of his body armour in the near future, so he changed his mind

144

and pulled out of the deal. It was a sagacity move on the part of the SPAM, for of course he would need his body armour in the near future if he wanted to stay alive through the war the daft bastard. The thing that I noticed with the SPAMs was that everywhere they went, no matter how far the distance, they always got fully dressed with their body armour, webbing and helmets on. The SPAMs took no chances any more especially after getting their arses kicked in the Vietnam War and having so many fatalities; unlike us Brits, we only took our Gat and NBC kit with us around our location.

29

Everyone in our Node started to mount their vehicles, so I shook the SPAM's hand and wished him luck with his efforts in the war because nobody knew what would happen over here in the desert, including the SPAMs. Our Node made its way back to our location on the order of end ex. It was getting dark, and we had to drive with our headlights off with just our convoy lights on. This was great, and we really had to concentrate on the way we drove. We tried to stay in a straight line with just our convoy lights on, following behind vehicle by vehicle. We followed the little white spot of a convoy light of the vehicle in front. This could be a nightmare at times especially if the vehicle in front of us went down a ditch, and we had no clue where they'd gone because of the darkness. Even though we couldn't see the desert ground, I could tell the surface was extremely uneven by the way the vehicle's convoy light in front of us jumped all round the place. Even though we didn't do much today except drive, I felt calm and tired on our return back to our location.

Once Jim and I parked our Land Rovers under the cam-net, we grabbed our webbing and Gats and headed straight to our tent. Jay wasn't far behind. We sat up for a little bit and wrote a few more bluey's. As soon as Jay turned off the light, we heard a rustling noise, "What the fuck is that?" Jay asked as he reached up from his bed and switched the tent's light back on.

When the light came on the noise stopped, and we couldn't see what made the noise, so Jay switched the light off again. Once the light was off the noise came back, so Jay switched on the light and the noise stopped again. This was bothersome and wonderment, so I grabbed a torch as Jay switched the light off. The noise started again, and I shone the torch's light in the direction of where the noise was coming from. Oddly, it came from beneath my camp cot. In the torches beam of light, stood a frozen desert rat that was chewing away on an empty Twix Chocolate bar wrapper. Jay and Jim picked up their boots and started chucking them at the terrified desert rat. "Leave it alone, yeah bastards! Its done fuck all to yous," I shouted at them.

They just laughed as they reached for more items of kit to chuck at the rat as it was quickly darting around the tent in a frenzied state. In the end,

I managed to corner the poor thing. It was a cute little rodent, and there was no way I could let any harm come to it. As I went to pick it up by its tail, the rodent gave out a gaudily high-pitched screech and ran off, leaving its tail in my right thumb and index finger. I was stunned, and Jay and Jim nearly fell off of their cots with fits of laughter, "I guess it won't be coming back in this tent in a hurry," Jim laughed, and he switched the tents light off.

The next day was another glorious day, weather wise, and the day gave me the perfect opportunity to do my dobhi. In addition, we were told that we would move to 7 Brigade HQ tomorrow. Jay had the same idea as me, and he washed his clothes too. As for Jim, I can't remember the last time he emptied his dhobi bag. Since we strictly dealt with radio sets, I placed the set's batteries on charge again to make sure the sets were in perfect working order. In the evening, after our dobhi had been done, and after the whole Node had eaten, we were finally issued with our British Army CBA from the Q.

We had to put the body armour together ourselves. The body armour came in two parts, the green body armour and the desert DPM outer cover. It was a right awkward bastard to get the armour inside its cover, and I didn't like the idea of us getting issued with body armour. We were Royal Signals, and I felt that we didn't need any kind of body armour because we'd be so far back from the front line that we'd might as well stayed in Germany. That was the general idea, but past conflicts proved anything could happen in war. We were getting deep into the true aspects of war, but when I received a bank statement today, which was for the end of January, it stated my balance was £890; it brought me back to some kind of reality. I suppose being out here had its advantages; however, I packed away most of my kit and readied for tomorrow.

When I arose the next day, the Node started to make its move to 7 Brigade's HQ at ten o'clock in the morning, and we were told that we'd be on the move for a couple of hours. 7 Brigade was much further north than our present location. Every time we moved location it was in a northern direction. Eventually, we joined up with 043, who were also being deployed to 7 Brigade. Now, numerous amounts of the Division's Trunk Nodes were being deployed to both the 7 and 4 Brigade to provide Ptarmigan comms whenever needed. When we arrived at 7 Brigade's location, various other units were already there and had set up their own little location within the brigade. This location was much the same as all the others, sand, sand and more sand. Sergeant Clay lead our Node to where we would set up our location, and, finally, I felt that I was going to be doing what I was trained to do; work the sets. For without radios, there would be no communications between divisions, which would play a vital and important part in the forthcoming land war. Sergeant Clay pointed to the spot where he wanted me to position my 1-Tonnie.

The wagons of our Node were positioned in a triangular formation. My 1-Tonnie and Jim's 110 Land Rover took up the top point, leading the way for the rest of the Node to place their wagons as directed by Sergeant Clay. All the Relay's lined up down my left, all the admin wagons formed the base of the triangle behind, and the Switch, Node Command, along with the Tech's wagons were positioned on my right to form the third side of the triangle. Once all the vehicles were camouflaged under their cam-nets, we dug our shell scrapes, which was a shallow trench to protect us all from shrapnel. The shell scrape was the length of your body with the depth of the trench, ranging from one and a half feet at the top and to two feet at the bottom. This allowed the rain to drain quickly to the bottom. It took me twenty minutes to complete and finished my last dig, and, then, Jay came round with the mail.

I received my Valentine card from Paula at long last. It came just in the nick of time with it being St. Valentines Day tomorrow. The card broadened a smile to my face when I opened the envelope. I was joyfully over the moon with delight; in addition, it was a huge personal morale boost, which was much needed at the time. The card also contained a letter from Paula telling me she was struggling a bit financially and was skint. I also received a letter from Phil Rotherham, who was a technician based at RAF Brize Norton with 244 Signal Squadron. I used to be at 8 Sigs in Catterick with him, and I used to give him ten pounds for a lift to Liverpool and back every weekend leave. The strange thing with Phil was that he used to be in the R.A.F. and decided that he had had enough of being a 'Brylcream Boy' and instead wanted to be a squaddie and transferred to the army. I had never met anyone who had transferred inter service before. He was also a fellow Evertonian and sent me the latest issue of the Everton fanzine magazine, 'When Skies are Grey.' One of the lads came round and informed Jay and I that we would be moving again tomorrow, so we immediately grabbed this opportunity to reply to our latest influx of mail.

There was a bit of trouble tonight at tea, for Staff Large told the Relay lads that the slop jockeys wouldn't be cooking for them anymore, and that they would have to fend for themselves. This meant they had to live off of ten-man ration packs while all us admin lads had the well-favoured privilege of much better and fresher rations. This course of action by Staff Large brought a rift between the Relay and admin lads, effectively splitting the Node in half. It was a good job there wasn't a trade union within the army because those Relay lads would have downed their rifles and went on strike. I went to bed that evening wandering how Staff Large's latest decision over eating would have an effect on the Node in the forthcoming months.

The whole Node was woken as dawn broke. We ate breakfast first, minus the Relay lads before packing up, and, then, Jim and I were put on pan bash duty. On the brighter side while we were washing the pots and pans, we were given our pay slips by Staff Large and I saw that our two percent pay raise that Maggie Thatcher, our previous Prime Minister had awarded us had been included in this months pay. Maggie Thatcher gave the British Armed Forces a massive pay rise last April before she resigned as Prime Minister last November. This pay rise was the first part of two part 12% pay rise with the remaining 10% due to be paid to us this forthcoming April. Still, this made our wages not quite worthwhile, for we didn't get paid enough to risk our lives for foreigners. After pan bash Jim and I got on with packing our kit away and the whole Node were all packed up and ready to move on by 11:00 am.

30

Sergeant Clay had come round all the wagons and informed us that we would be following 043. "What are we doing now, Trev?" I asked Sergeant Clay.

"We will be practising going through the breech over the next few days," he replied.

The drive wasn't long before we came to our first stop, which was the start point of our rehearsal with all the British Army units that took part last time. I drove down to 043 to see Danny Steele. We talked for a while, and he gave me a can of coke and a Mars bar, which he had received in a parcel from his mam. When I returned to my position, Sergeant Clay gave me a right bollocking for taking my 1-Tonnie down the line, "Where the fuck have you been? This Rover isn't yours to go joy riding, Molloy!"

It was alright for him to use it as a personnel taxi, I thought to myself. "I hope yeah get taken out by an Iraqi shell, yeah fucking prick!" I muted out of earshot.

Lieutenant Naden came round the Node and called us all in for a briefing. He gave the brief on where all the Nodes would get dropped off and located once we crossed the breach for real. 043 would be dropped off first, and we, 053, would be the last to get dropped off in the deepest of enemy territory. This shitted me up a little bit. But, at this point, I looked around and saw the expression on the lad's faces mixed with some showing fear and others not flickering a wink. It was just my luck to be in the node that got the one-way ticket to hell. Once Lieutenant Naden finished with the brief, we were ordered to go back to our vehicles and get some shuteye because we didn't know when we would get the order to move out.

I did manage to get a few hours sleep and it was pitch black and just after midnight as the vehicle packets started to roll out. There would be VHF comms on this exercise with Jim and I doing six-hour radio shifts between the two of us. During the night, we moved so fast that we didn't have time to stop, and I knew that I would be doing a longer shift than agreed upon, but that's just the way things went. The sun had risen before we stopped for the foreseeable future, which would be our new location. Jim took over for me on shift whilst it was my turn to help cam the

Danny Steele getting his NBC kit on.

vehicles. I placed Hessian over the window screens and mirrors to stop the sun's reflection and not give away our new location. In a short while, I took back over for Jim because his six hours were up, and it also got me out from digging the shell scrapes. This little job fell on hard to Jim before he could even relax. OSC 135 moved into our location to join us in this part of the exercise and with them they brought our mail.

We were lucky to receive mail today with being on the exercise, and I received a letter from my mam. She didn't have much to say, but I replied to her; furthermore, I wrote to Paula and to my bank when I took over from Jim on shift. The reason why I wrote to my bank was to cancel the standing order of one hundred and fifty pounds to Paula's account, because she was spending it instead of saving it for our wedding. I had set up the standing order when I was last home on leave. However, I couldn't control what she did, for I was in the middle of the fucking desert, so with me not being able to spend my money; I thought it best that the money remained in my bank account. Since I had been on shift reading my mail and writing bluey's, no radio traffic had come across the net (*Combat Net Radio - CNR - group of call signs belonging to a unit working on the same frequency).*

Seemingly, it was a waste of time to keep the VHF and HF comms open because there hadn't been any radio traffic and we were now static. When the Ptarmigan is up and running, there is no reason to use the CNR. Once Jim came to take over from me on shift, I had to go and stag on with Wilkie. The time on this stag sluggishly dragged on, and it didn't help being bored off my tits listening to nothing on the sets all day. Half way through our stag, we noticed the lights of planes heading northward in the night sky. We continued to trace their movements until we lost eye contact, nevertheless, we both kept looking in that direction, and about five minutes later there were a few orange glows on the horizon. "Fuck me! I bet some poor bastard is getting a right hammering," I told Wilkie.

"We can't be that far from the border," Wilkie replied.

I kept on thinking about how far we actually were from the border of Iraq, maybe twenty to thirty miles away at most. I was made up when our relief came because I was tired and just couldn't keep my eyes open much longer. I knew that I would only get a few hours of sleep before Jim came and nudged me to take over from him again. But, a few hours of sleep were better than none at all. When I came off shift in the early morning, Jim informed me that we were moving to 'Area Ray' today. Area Ray was the code name given by the British Army for an area of the Saudi desert close to the Iraqi border that would be used as a maintenance area for her troops and all last minute preparations. It was a nice day for a drive, considering how hot it got. The journey to 'Area Ray' took us past the city of Hafar Al Batin and through a desolate desert valley. Hafar Al Batin would be our last sight of civilization as it would be all deserts from here onwards. The sand sunk in very soft in parts, and my 1-Tonnie got bogged down into the sand again. "These Rovers are fucking shite!" I screamed at the top of my voice. It doesn't help matters if the army can't get you the parts you need to fix it either. The admin Bedford had to come and pull me free with its winch, and by the time this had been achieved the rest of the node had fucked far off into the distance. I put my foot down and agilely raced to catch up the rest of the Node. The Node halted on the other side of the brow of the sandy hill. We waited a couple of minutes for the admin Bedford to catch up before we set off again as an entire Node. The time took us the best part of the day to reach our destination. On the way, we drove past a field ambulance location to get to where our Node would be located. All of 7

12-2-91

Hey up GONK.

Its nice to hear From you again
i Bet you got a right shock when our Darren
told you that I cos Pregnant. what was our
Darrens reactions to the her, was he pleased
about it, or was he mad. Alan is very pleased
about becoming a Dad its posed to be due
on the 6th August that makes me 4 monts. i Dont
think Alan can wait that Long. were not getting
married Just yet but i have put my name down
For a house at the council office, so when
the babys born and i get a house Alan will
be Living with me and if we are still getting
on allright then we will get married. what
Do you mean Alan must be hard up to have me?
ill kill you when i See you. Are me and alan,
me mam + Len all invited to your wedding
next year, if you buy me something For the
baby i might think of buying you a wedding
present.
        me mam wants to know if our Darren's
allright because he never writes in his letters
how he is. i will have to go now.
                Sonia.

P.S. please write back and Let us all
how how you and our Darren. is
P.P.S i couldent call my Dog Peter. HaHa.

Bluey I received from Sonia Steele.

154

Brigade's units were located here before the big push. The slop jockeys put on a late meal once we set up our location. After tea, I headed straight to bed because tomorrow was going to be a busy day.

The next morning I awoke early, and this day was the first day of a week long maintenance programme for everyone in the British Army from vehicles to personnel kit before the land faze of the war started. I worked on my 1-Tonnie, starting with my radio batteries, checking each and every cell very carefully to ensure the battery acid levels hadn't dropped. They were fine, so I dusted them down and took the old grease off the terminals and replaced it with fresh PX 7 grease. Jay spent all day checking my five hundred-watt generator, but he couldn't get it started. None of my kit worked properly. While det commanders were working on their wagons the rest of the lads were busy digging a couple of trenches at both ends of our location for stag duty. The day just seemed full of, but necessary bull shit. On the other hand, it was a good day, for we got another load of mail in, and I received a bluey from Sonia.

Sonia had written this letter on the 12th of February and referred to me as 'Gonk', which I thought must have been a Yorkshire saying. She said it was nice to hear from me again and that she and her boyfriend, Alan, were made up with having a baby. She also said she had put her name down for a council house for her and Alan. She made me laugh when I read the P.P.S. at the bottom of her bluey that said she wouldn't call her dog Peter, which was her response to my suggestion of naming her baby after me. Sonia lived in a town called Hemsworth, which is in West Yorkshire. I've been up to Sonia's house a few times to visit. It would take a few hours by National Express coach from Liverpool to Pontefract with a change at Leeds. Once I got into Pontefract, which was the closest coach station to Hemsworth, I would then get a bus for the final six and a half miles into Hemsworth. The main reason why I used to keep in touch with Sonia when I came out of the juniors was because I used to fancy her, but nothing ever came of it. Once I finished reading Sonia's bluey, I turned my attention to the bluey I received from Paula.

She said in her bluey how sorry she was for having the abortion and how she would like to try for another baby whenever I got home. Whether she felt guilty for what she had done or not, I didn't know. I wrote straight back to her. To put her at ease, I told her that I was alright now, and there was no need for us to try for another baby until we were both ready. I felt that if we tried for a baby when I got back, it would be for all the wrong reasons. I also wrote to my mate's back at home to let them know what I was up to now without giving anything away about the war, not that I really knew what the fuck was going on anyway. Jay placed an orange light in our tent, so it would help us write when it went dark. It came in handy to have a powerman living with me in our tent.

The sun was so hot today that a few of us lads wore no T-shirts, but only our body armour. Staff Large alertly noticed this, came over and gave us five extras for being improperly dressed.

"Get your T-shirts on now and go see Corporal Tuff. And, tell him how many extras you've got," he ordered us.

"Yes, Staff," we said reluctantly.

Jay popped his head out of the tent to see what all the commotion was all about.

"What a fucking wanker that bloke is," I exclaimed to Jay has I stormed off to see Gaz Tuff. I cooled off a bit by the time I had gotten to Gaz. I let him know what just happened and the extras I was given. Gaz was in charge of the stag list at our trench.

"Don't worry, Scouse. You won't be doing them, we know how much of a wanker he is," Gaz reassured me.

I thanked Gaz for the favour, and I thought that this is what the army should be about, people looking out for one another and not trying to fuck them about. I didn't see the point of us doing guards here when we had the Artillery's Javelin sites dotted all round the brigade's location. The Javelin was short range, man portable anti-armour missile and was ideal for close air defence.

31

I had another VHF comms exercise today with all the other Nodes. The good thing about this exercise was the fact it was static. The purpose of this exercise was to check out our pineapple kit again, just to double check. There were only five call signs on the net giving radio checks to one another to test transmitting and receive capability. Once everyone had comms with each other, the YoS, who was responsible for all comms in the field, came on the net and called end ex. Only being able to do these little bits of radio operating was pissing me off, so once I had stowed away my antenna kit, I took a walk over to Node Command to have a word with Lieutenant Naden.

"Excuse me, sir. Is it all right to have a word with yeah a sec, please?" I asked him politely.

"Yes. Sure, Molloy. Come in," he said.

"What it is sir; Jay Curly and me are still not happy here, and we would like to know if we can get a move to brigade?" I asked.

I also told him that Staff Large was not just pissing me off but also a lot of the troop as well, and I can't handle being in the same place has him. He told me that there would be no chance with everyone preparing to cross the breach. I really hated it here with half the senior rank pricks in this Node. Disheartened by Lieutenant Naden's response to my request to be transferred I slowly walked back to my tent releasing my frustration by kicking the tyre tracks in the sand and scattering grains of sand across the desert floor.

While the weather was still on my side, I decided to get my dobhi from my tent and get rid of my stockpile of my dirty clothes that had built up. This could be the last time I would get the opportunity for a long while, and it won't do going into battle without clean underwear on. The worse thing about doing my dobhi was cleaning it without washing powder. I had to use my block of 'Shield' hand soap to clean my clothes as well as my body. I draped my now Shield fresh clothes on the cam net to dry as this was the best use for them in this flat desert wilderness. As I hung up my last pair of boxer shorts, one of the lads shouted over that there was going to be a briefing in ten minutes at OSC 135, and we all had to attend.

Every member form the brigade's Nodes who weren't on essential duty were at this briefing. We all gathered round the entrance of a cam netted tent and vehicles with a notice board out side covered with a big sheet of white paper. OSC 135's OC came out from beneath the cam net and started the briefing off with, "You will not take any notes or write anything down you hear today in your bluey's back home. Do you understand?"

"Sir!" we all enthusiastically shouted back at him.

He stood to the left hand side of the board and pulled the sheet of white paper over the back of the board to reveal the plan of the allied forces invasion of Iraq and the liberation of Kuwait. I stood in amazement with what was in front of my eyes on the board. It was a rough diagram on a clear plastic sheet with Saudi Arabia to the south, Iraq to the north and Kuwait to the Northeast. Under Kuwait were the joint Arab forces and backed up by some American units of their 3rd Army. Their job was to fight back the occupying Iraqi forces and liberate Kuwait. Above those forces was an arrow of their advance into Kuwait. Inside Kuwait it was believed there was a position of an Iraqi armoured division. "Gentlemen, this is where we are interested in," the OC said has he pointed across the Iraqi/Kuwaiti border into Iraq and continued, "To the south of Iraq on the border with Saudi Arabia is a dark thick line," the OC said in a quizzing manner whilst resting his finger on the dark thick line.

The dark line ran along the border of Kuwait/Saudi Arabia on the East Coast through the Iraqi/Kuwait border half way into Iraq. We had already heard about this line on the news.

"This dark line represents a trench, which is filled with oil, and it is believed that Saddam will set it a light to prevent the invasion," the OC informed us and continued with his brief, "Just north of the Saudi border with Iraq are two Iraqi mechanised brigades. To the left of their position is where we will advance through the breach using a left flanking attack. This to wipe out these brigades here and here, and we will also take out any retreating Iraqi forces trying to flee Kuwait." He paused for a second after pointing out the positions of the Iraqi mechanised brigades, and then continued. "There will be the 1st American Division and us, the 1st British Armoured Division going through this passage here," he said sternly, pointing to the Iraqi/Saudi border, where the Big Red One will spearhead the breach of the Iraqi defences.

And, he went on, "The Americans will take out the first Iraqi brigade here, and, then, we will leap frog them and take out the second brigade here by the Iraqi/Kuwaiti border. We will advance straight through their positions and form a Div HQ, and that gentleman will be the end of the war for the British. Further to the North and left will be the American 89th Airborne Division and the French Foreign Legion. Their job is to stop any re-supply to the Iraqi forces. That's all the information I am able to give you at this point. Are they're any questions?" The OC asked.

Nobody asked any relevant questions, I think everyone was in a state of shock that it was becoming more real and that this was serious business. As soon as has there were no more questions, the OC dismissed us back to our Nodes.

When I returned back to the Node, Jay had finally managed to get my generator working, "About time, ain't it? If yeah weren't skiving all day, yeah could have had it working ages ago," I said jokingly.

"Fuck off, yeah cunt," he mumbled under his breath.

Since my generator was up and running, I disconnected the radio batteries out of my 1-Tonnie and placed them on charge. Once this was done, I went to get my last hair cut from Staff Large, which will be a grade one all over. I didn't know when the next opportunity would arise. I returned back to my wagon to clear it out because I had a lot planned for tomorrow.

A banging and uncanny thumping noise came from outside the tent, which woke us all up. Jay went outside to investigate what made the loud noise. There was a ferocious wind outside, and it had blown down one of the cam net poles, and it had struck the 1-Tonnie. It started to rain very heavy, and all my kit along with Sergeant Clay's was outside getting pissed wet through. I looked at my watch, and it was 4:30am, and there was no way I was getting out of my warm doss bag to become cold and wet. If that wasn't enough, our tent was starting to lift up and flap about in the wind. Jay grabbed the mallet and ran round the outside of our tent hammering the pegs back into the sand whilst Jim and I fought with the storm to keep the tent on the deck. Once the tent was safe and secure, we managed to get some more sleep.

32

Once the sun arose, we could see the furious and tempest devastation that last night's storm caused round us. There were cam nets just draped over the vehicles with the poles just thrown about the desert. Some of the pegs that held the cam nets in position had been uprooted as well. I turned to see what my kit was like. I had imagined it would be like pissed wet through. To my surprise, as I opened my Bergen, all my kit inside was dry. The news wasn't that good though when I opened my kit and travel bags. Everything inside was damp, so as soon as we had sorted out our cam net, I hung all my clothes out to dry. There was nothing else for me to do, so while I was waiting for everything to dry, I went to the admin tent to watch a video.

There were quite a few of the lads already in the admin tent watching videos. A recording of 'Blind Date' was on, and it made me slightly home sick. Not because of Cilla Black - the show's presenter who comes from Liverpool - but one of the couples from the previous week had won their blind date in Liverpool. They went all round the Albert Dock, which was where Paula and I always went to on a Sunday afternoon for a walk and a drink. I was on a bit of downer until the mail came in, and I received a bluey from Paula and another one from a mate back home. I went back to my tent to read and reply when I was handed another three bluey's from Paula. I was getting pissed off with her as I started to read them. As I was reading through them, all Paula was going on about again was having a baby when I got back home and how sorry she was for the abortion. For all the blueys she'd sent, this was all she had wrote about recently, and I wasn't even going to finish the fourth one when something she wrote brought a smile to my face. She wrote that she would have to appear in court for none payment of Poll Tax back from when she was living with her parents. I burst into fits of laughter. It's a good job I cancelled my standing order to her bank account because she would have probably paid her fine with my money. This bluey certainly changed my morale for the better.

To pass a bit of time before going to bed, I thought it best to give my Gat a good clean. I couldn't recall the last time I put my pull-through down its barrel. When I removed the top cover of my Gat, the entire working parts were coated in the Arabian Desert. When I removed my magazines from my webbing's ammo (*ammunition*) pouches to give them a clean, they too were in a sorry state. I emptied all the rounds out of the magazines and stripped them down to give them a well-deserved dusting down. Good job my life hadn't been relying on my Gat since I last cleaned it. It had taken me just over an hour to bring it up to serviceability. As I was putting my Gat back together again, Jay strutted into the tent, clutching a fist full of Bluey's, "I've got a load of bluey's from pen pigs here. I'll read them tomorrow cos I can't be arsed now," he said casually.

My wagon needed my full attention today with only days to go. I took my radio batteries off charge and connected them back up to the sets. Sandy was spending his day working on my 1-Tonnie. He was trying to make a temporary repair to the 4-wheel drive, but there wasn't much he could do with out the replacement parts. It looks like I'm going into war with a fucked 1-Ton Land Rover. Just has Sandy was packing away his tools, the word was given for everyone to get into NBC stage two. Therefore, I raced to my side pouch of my Bergen to start getting dressed into my NBC suit. As I finished fastening my NBC jacket, Jay came into the tent.

"Iraq has just launched five Scud Missiles, but the worse thing is that nobody knows where they are heading," Jay said worriedly.

I went over to the guard post, for it was my turn to stag on, and as I strolled over to do my stag, I looked up into the dusk sky. Dusk and dawn were the best times of the day for one force to attack another. The reason behind this was that a person's eyesight hadn't had time to adjust between the transitional periods of natural light. There were plenty of our allied planes heading north too, but we had no reports of yet that Scuds were heading in the opposite direction. I relieved Dave for the next two hours. I had my CND (*Campaign for Nuclear Disarmament*) head on for the duration of the stag, thinking what the fuck I was doing over here. It went through my mind for ages as I asked myself, "Why should I die for these Packi bastards? This isn't even my country?"

I wasn't being a coward. It was just that I didn't mind fighting for Queen and country if my country was in direct threat. I just can't comprehend dying for somebody else's country. The war was affecting my mind, but I managed to change my attitude when I came off stag when I learnt that Saddam had targeted Israel with his Scuds. I couldn't believe it because Israel wasn't even in this war, and it turned me back

162

into a bloodthirsty squaddie who wanted to kill every Iraqi in sight. Jay also informed me that there was going to be last minute panegyrics and peace talks tomorrow between the Soviet Union and Iraq. The only Soviet involvement in this war was one of peace broker between the allied countries and Iraq.

I thought it was best if I took care of some personal admin today just in case the peace talks on this particular day failed, and we would have to start the land war in a couple of days. Sandy came round as I was hanging up my washing on the cam nets to dry. "Alright, Scouse have you heard, the peace talks have failed and that we are moving to the holding area on Sunday at two o'clock p.m.," he informed me.

All I could think about was that it would be all out war from now on, with no turning back. No amount of training I had received could prepare me for what lay ahead. The time had now come for me to grow up big time and start acting like a man and except what was to happen in the very near future. I checked that my kit was dry and I made sure that I packed my kit with the most essential items such as spare NBC suits and ammunitions being very accessible. Once this had been done I was nervous, but prepared for Sunday. So, I put pen to paper, and I first wrote to my mam.

"Dear Mum, I've just found out today that we are going in on Sunday. I don't know when you'll receive this bluey, but hopefully, I'll be alright. I don't know what lies ahead for us, and if I die, I don't want any of you fighting at my funeral. You can't blame my dad, and he can't blame you. Take care, lots of love, Pete."

I wrote more or less the same to my dad. Since my mother walked out on my dad when I was nine years old, they hadn't really gotten on with one another. If I were to die, there would be the hostilities. The bluey I wrote to Paula was more of a personal and sloppy one. I was hoping there would be a phone run tomorrow or the day after, so I could make one last call to Paula, simply because it could be the last time I would hear her voice, and the last time I would have had to tell her I loved her. That night, I fell asleep wandering what laid ahead for me.

There were only a few loose ends on my 1-Tonnie that I had to sort out before the move tomorrow. Staff Large came round to everyone and ordered us to open a new NBC suit. Staff Large took everyone's old NBC suit and buried them in the desert. I could feel the butterflies in my stomach starting to flutter and rattling nerves as well. This was definitely it; I was going to war tomorrow. The word was passed round that there would be a few phone runs on this evening to the city of Hafar Al Batin. I managed to get myself on the first trip with another seven lads.

When we arrived in the city it was early evening and still light and I saw it was a shit hole compared to western standards. We were all given a time of a couple of hours to report back to the Land Rover before setting off in search of some change for the phones. We tried to get change in the way of coins for the phones from the shops, but it was pointless. They mostly gave us change in sweets rather than mess with coins. We asked a young Arab lad, who looked about 18, where the nearest bank was. His English was better than my Arabic, and he raised his arm and pointed us in the direction of the bank. We set off down one of the main streets, keeping an eye out for something that resembled a bank. The streets were deserted, and the way we all marched down the road and through the streets with the butt of our Gats in our shoulder resembled something out of a war film.

33

Most of the town's buildings were covered in a greyish plaster, but only the odd building had been given a lick of paint, which made them stand out from the rest of the buildings. They were like this on both sides of the road. When we came across the bank, it was totally different from all the other buildings we came across. The bank was a modern building with two security guards with rifles standing outside. One of the security guards wore a western style uniform whilst the other and older security guard who looked to me to be middle aged and unshaven, wore the traditional Thobe, which is a long sleeve, loose fitting, ankle length garment that was white in colour and made from cotton. On his head he wore a red and white shemagh with a silver, Saudi Arabian cross swords and palm tree emblem cap badge pinned to the agal. The agal is a thick double piece of black cord that prevents the shemagh from slipping off the head. I entered the bank, which was quite posh inside, and I asked the man behind the counter if he had any coins that I could exchange for riyal notes. He didn't have any, and I was feeling well pissed off that I might not get the chance to phone Paula before going to war. We made our way back to the Land Rover to meet up with the others. And when everyone was accounted for, we took a drive down to a service station to get something to eat and hopefully some change. As I was climbing over the tailboard of the Land Rover, a British squaddie came out of the shop.

"Have yeah got any spare change on yeah; mate, so I can use the phone?" I asked him.

"Sorry, I haven't mate. But if you go into the hotel next door, they'll let you use their phones and settle up once you've finished," he let me know.

After I heard that, I let the lads know and made a beeline straight for the hotel. As I entered the lobby of the hotel, which was not very big, there was a three seater couch immediately on my right and immediately to my front, about twenty five feet from the front door of the hotel were three telephone cubicles with glass panels in the top half of the cubicle doors. To the right of the telephone cubicles was a stairwell that led to the hotel bedrooms and to my left was a black man standing behind the reception desk. "Alright, mate is there any chance I could use your phone, please?" I asked in desperation.

"Yes, you can. I charge eleven riyals a minute," he replied in very good

English.

I took all my money out of my pocket and placed it down on the reception desk to count and I had one hundred and twenty riyals on me, which would give me ten agonizing minutes as this could be the last time I ever spoke to the woman I love.

"Yeah, that's sound," I told him as I gave him Paula's work number.

The receptionist dialed Paula's work number and when he had the ring tone he directed me to the second cubicle where he patched the call to. I open the cubicle door and entered the 3'x 3' cubicle and closed the door behind me. Inside the cubicle on the wall above the telephone was a list of the international dialing codes for every country. I picked the hand set up and placed it to my left ear whilst looking out of the cubicle into the empty lobby area. The phone rang for about fifteen seconds before someone answered.

It was Paula that answered the phone; how lucky was that? I was made up to hear her voice again and the line was crystal clear. We didn't know what to really say to each other; therefore, we just made light conversation. I told her that it could be awhile before I would be able to call her again because I couldn't exactly tell her we were going to invade Iraq the next day. The phone line wasn't secure and anybody could have been eavesdropping in on the conversation. It came up to the ten-minute mark as I told her, "I'll have to go now, love. Love yeah."

"I love you too, ta-ra," she replied.

I wished I could have spoken to her for much longer, but I was grateful with the opportunity of that short phone call. Once I placed the handset back on the receiver, I paused for a second to gather my composure then made my way to the reception desk to settle my bill for the phone call. The receptionist told me my call cost one hundred riyals, which worked out to around sixteen pounds. Everyone was waiting on me when I returned to the Land Rover. I told them about the hotel and the phone, and that I'd have to tell the next load of lads on the next phone run when we returned back to our location.

When we returned back to our location, it was dark and the other Rover was filling up with the next phone run. Flinnie was walking towards me shaking his head as I got out of the back of the Rover.

"What's up Flinnie, la?" I asked.

"Mr. Naden has just ordered me to go on the phone run to phone Vicky. She's gone into camp back in Germany and told the family's officer that

Flinnie on a rare occasion writing a bluey to his wife.

I've hardly called nor wrote to her," he informed me.

I nearly pissed myself with laughter as Flinnie continued to tell me that a signal had been sent from our camp in Germany for the attention of Lieutenant Naden and for Lieutenant Naden to order Signalman Flintham to make a phone call back home. Flinnie hadn't appreciated his wife's concerning enquiry at the family's office into his lack of communication with her. The look of bewilderment on Flinnie's face was clear for all to see as he couldn't see what all the fuss was about. It was true though that Flinnie hardly ever went on a phone run, so I supposed anybody couldn't really blame his wife going into camp to find out some information. I headed straight to my tent still in fits of laughter. And when I walked in, I saw Jay was writing some bluey's.

"I've just seen Flinnie, and he's just been ordered to go and phone his tart up by Lieutenant Naden," I told him.

Jay doubled over, and we both had a good laugh at Flinnie's expense. I left Jay writing his bluey's when I went to bed.

It's Sunday the 24th of February 1991, and this was the day our war started, and the history books had gotten a bit of fresh input. The weather wasn't too good with a slight sandstorm popping up. I was on top of my wagon packing away the cam net when a big gush of wind caught me from behind and knocked me off balance. I fell off the top of my wagon

Me posing just before the land invasion of Iraq, Saudi Arabia, February 1991.

and landed on the desert floor with a thud on my back. I couldn't move for a while as I had the wind knocked out of me, but has soon as the shock was over and I could breath steadily, I picked myself up and dusted myself down just as Sergeant Clay was heading in my direction.

"Hey Scouse, Corporal Marriott will be your co-driver, alright?" Sergeant Clay shouted over to me.

Sam Marriott walked over to see me about the co-driver's job. "Hey, Sam, I hear you can't drive. Is it true?" I asked him.

"Yeah, that's right, Scouse," he replied with a big sadistic smile on his face.

Jay writing his final letters home and to pen pigs before crossing the breach.

That was just great, fancy sending me a co-driver who couldn't drive. Sam was a loon at the best of times without him being not able to drive.

"Well, it's about time yeah learnt. I'll give yeah your first lesson now, so jump in," I told him.

He jumped in behind the steering wheel with excitement as I thought now would be the best time for him to learn with the rest of the Node still packing up. I started with the basics with him. A 1-Ton Land Rover was not the ideal vehicle to teach someone to drive. The 1-Tonnie was a left hand drive with manual gears. I explained to him that the left foot pedal is the clutch and that he had to dip the clutch to place the vehicle into gear and to change gears; the middle pedal is the brake, which had to be used in conjunction with the clutch when bring the vehicle to a halt to prevent the engine from stalling and the right pedal is the accelerator and also had to be used in conjunction with the clutch when first moving the vehicle to allow a smooth start. Also, I explained to Sam that it was important for him not to have his left foot on the clutch when driving as this would damage the clutch. Once he was familiar with the pedals I then showed him how to operate the indicators and head lights. I told Sam to start the engine then check the mirrors to ensure there was no traffic, indicate which direction he was going and when it was clear to move off. He started off alright with the odd kangaroo jump as he didn't get the timing right between the clutch and the accelerator, but soon settled down. I let him drive around the location while slowly moving up the gears, so he could get used to the gear stick and changing gears. I let him drive around in circles for twenty minutes, so I was happy he could handle the 1-Tonnie. Sam was made up with his little driving lesson and gave a sadistic giggle as he thanked me and jumped out of the driver's seat. The Node was packed up and ready to move when we were called over to join the packet. The Node formed up in one packet waiting on the order for us to move.

Just as the sun was setting, our Node received the signal to move. The whole brigade must have been told at the same time because everywhere you looked there were packets of vehicles on the move. Most of the wagons had Union Jacks flying from them. I wished I had brought mine out here with me instead of packing it away in my MFO box. It gave me a great buzz and again made me proud to be British. I switched the red fog light on, which was above my wagon's back door. Some might think this to be strange, going into combat in the dark with a bright red light shining all over the place. The reasons for the red lights was so our bombers and fighter planes, mainly the SPAMs, could distinguish their own forces from the enemy and not have a 'blue on blue', in other words getting attacked by our own forces. As we drove along the tracks to where the brigade would be forming up they were lit up by red and green chemical lights.

These lights served the purpose so the wheeled vehicles didn't get mixed up with the tracked vehicles. The wheeled vehicles like Land Rovers stayed to the left of the red lights and the tracked vehicles stayed to the right. There were plenty of tracked vehicles like Challenger 1 main battle tanks, Warriors and 436 Royal Signals armoured radio personnel carrier as well as armoured ambulances. There were all kinds of vehicles, and seeing and hearing them all was very exciting. After about an hour's drive we arrived at the staging area and we were moved into position by the RMP, staying in our packets. When we stopped, every one automatically jumped out of the vehicles and started digging shell scrapes. We had reached the holding area; that is this would be our last position before we crossed the breach into Iraq.

34

The POL pod Bedford from the RCT came down to our packet to fill all the wagon's fuel tanks, so that when we were half way across the breach, we didn't run out of fuel. I needed to fill my 1-Tonnie as it guzzles the fuel like it was going out of fashion. Now, I was getting really excited, and the adrenaline was starting to race around my body, for the unknown was about. I looked around me in the pitch-black night with the only light coming from the stars, and I could see the terrain was a bit bumpy. All of a sudden, we saw a few bright flashes and heard a whooshing sound off in the distance. The Artillery's MLRS (*Multiple Launch Rocket System*) had fired off a few of its rockets towards the Iraqi positions just inside the Iraqi border. This was to soften the enemy up before we went through their positions.

"Fucking hell! Did yeah see that!" I shouted excitedly to Sam.

This was brilliant. The sights and sounds gave me a huge buzz. The fireworks display lasted for about a quarter of an hour, and when it was finished, I climbed up in my wagon and got my head down to sleep whilst I had the chance.

A big bang on the side of my 1-Tonnie roused me awake. It was now seven thirty in the morning, and Sam was already up and dressed. We were told by Sergeant Clay to be ready to move for eight-fifteen in the morning and dressed in NBC stage three, which the difference between stage two was that stage three included our S10 respirator. It was a dull morning, and I made do with last night's rainwater to have a cold wash and shave. I didn't want to waste any drinking water just in case there was no chance of a re-supply once we got into Iraq. Once eight fifteen came, we were all ready to move; nonetheless, typical to the British Army, we didn't move on time. We just sat round. I fell asleep again behind the wheel and was woken up again at eleven o'clock in the morning, as we were now ready to move. The packets started to move slowly and gradually, stopping at times. This 'snail' momentum was really pissing me off. It soon came to light what was causing the delay, and it was all the packets formulating and moving off the desert onto one main track to cross the border. In the light of day the terrain was bumpy and I was bouncing up and down in my seat. When we eventually drove onto the track, we were still stopping at times. At this rate the war would

SPAM's on the move.

have been over before we left Saudi. As we drove further down the track there was a mound of sand, which ran away from both sides of the track across the desert. This mound of sand marked the border of Saudi Arabia and Iraq.

The mound of sand was about three feet high, and as we drove through the breach, there was a wooden sign pitched in the sand to the right of the track. The SPAMs had placed it there and painted black writing on it; welcome to occupied Iraq courtesy of the 'Big Red One,' with the SPAMs' unit's badge in the centre. The SPAMs were the first ones to cross the breach. This suited us fine as we thought they were more expendable than we were. At this point, I looked down at my speedometer and noticed that I had driven a very slow nine kilometers since the staging area. Finally, we crossed the border, and once inside the Iraqi border, the desert floor was extremely different from the desert floor just a few yards away on the other side of the border.

There were green patches of grass all over the Iraqi side in which I thought was very well weird because one side of the border was completely sand and the other green. Parts of the area were mine taped off either side of the track with SPAMs clearing these areas of mines. They must have had reports of this area being covered in mines, which was great insight to the Iraqi defences. Looking around, I couldn't see

British wagon with UH-60 Black Hawks transporting equipment to the left.

any signs of there being a firefight or even a war yet. I was expecting to see blown up burning vehicles and dead bodies strewn about the desert floor with all their limbs missing, but there was no such luck. What we had driven through was the 'Breach,' and it was perseveringly still going slow with all the vehicles passing through it. I didn't think anyone had a clue has to what was happening. When we first stopped, which was for about a minute, Sam and I swapped driving.

Sam's driving lesson must've worked, for he wasn't that bad the second time round at driving, and all the packets continued to head in the same direction including a few SPAM packets that joined the influx into Iraq. By now, we were driving through an Iraqi position that had already been cleared by the SPAMs during the night by the 'Big Red One.' We could see the Iraqi trenches and finally their burnt out vehicles, which were still ablaze. Invigoratingly, I was finally made up now. I thought I was going to go through the longevity of this war without seeing any kind of furious and pestilent destruction. There wasn't much to see, and the SPAMs must have cleaned up after themselves. I told Sam that it wouldn't be much of a war if it stayed like this. As Sam was driving along the track for wheeled vehicles, a 432-armoured ambulance cut straight across us and made us become separated from the rest of the Node. More 432 armoured ambulances followed that one, so Sam had to stop, and that caused the vehicles behind us to stop too, which halted the further penetration into Iraq. When Sam thought it was safe for us to cross the tracked vehicles track, he raced ahead to catch the rest of the Node up. All the Nodes had stopped about half a mile up the track when we arrived there. Staff Large came over to us and started to give me loads of shit for separating the packets as if it was my entire fault, and we had one hell of an argument. I told him that Sam was driving, and it wasn't his fault either. "Tiny is driving the one Tonnie now! And, your going in the relay wagon!" he shouted at me.

"It's my wagon, and I'm fucking driving it!" I hastily screamed back at him, pointing my finger at his chest.

"Shut the fuck up before I charge yeah," he retorted as the higher ranked NCO he was.

I legitimately turned away and docility went back to Sam. "I fucking hate that fat twat," I snarled at Sam.

I stayed in my wagon, but Tiny drove, and as we drove over hilly ground it started to rain. As the rain fell and the sand got soft, the 1-Tonnie began to get bogged in the sand. We finally came to a halt and had the ration and water Bedford with Staff Large behind us. The ration Bedford had a winch on it and it had to come round to pull us free. By the time this was done, the rest of the Node had vanished into the confusion of all the other vehicles. This was just great. All that was left of our Node were the ration Bedford, water bowser and my disabled 1-Tonnie, and because of the weather conditions my 1-Tonnie had to carry on being towed. Eventually, we latched onto another convoy, so we didn't get left behind. We didn't have a clue which unit it was or where they were heading; all we knew was that they were British. It turned dark again when the packet we were tagging along with stopped and set up their location. Staff Large went off to find out whom we were with and find out if he could find out where our Node was. Once he came back, he informed us that we were with 40-field battery, Royal Artillery. I asked Staff Large if I should go and find their command vehicle and try to get in touch with Jim, who was monitoring the VHF net. He agreed with the notion, so I grabbed my helmet and Gat and went off in search of hope.

I was off to see if I could get in touch with our Node on the Sigs Eng (*Signal Engineering*) Net and let them know where we were at although that was if they knew we were missing. After asking the Artillery's quartermaster, I found their command vehicle, and they were packing up

SPAM vehicles moving north.

and ready to move again. I turned round and ran back to my own vehicle, and when I arrived, Staff Large was giving the rest of the lads a brief. I could see who were left behind now. There was Staff Large, Sam, Hutch, Tiny, Sandy, Jay and me.

35

"The Stafford's and the Royal Scots Dragoon Guards have gone through their objectives, and we're going for the Republican Guard. And we are following right behind them," Staff Large finished as I arrived back.

Afterwards, we all jumped straight back into our wagons ready to carry on going forward. I kept on saying to myself that we were in the Royal Signals, and that we should be at the rear and not in the front chasing the infantry as they went to do battle with the enemy. Even though I had that cowardly thought, it still didn't prevent me from getting a little buzz of excitement from being affront. When we moved off again, I was still being towed by the ration Bedford, and we had to stop forty five minutes later. Staff Large jumped out of the cab of his ration wagon and approached my wagon.

"Right Molloy, I've just been told by the Artillery that we are slowing them down and there could be Iraqi tanks heading in our direction, so grab the radio kit and put it in the back of the ration Bedford and leave everything else behind. You've got five minutes," Staff Large ordered me.

I wasn't going to leave my personnel kit behind and just stay in the rest of the war in what I was standing in. Therefore, I went and grabbed Jay and Sam to give me a hand to unload my wagon. "Jay! Sam! Can yeah do us a favour and grab me personnel kit out of the back while I get the radios and that?" I asked them.

They started to unload my kit and take it to the ration Bedford and Tiny came over to help me unload the radios. "That's enough time now. Leave whatever else is there in the Rover," Staff Large demanded.

I was lucky I got my personnel kit, for that was more important than the radios to me. The 1-Tonnie had been disconnected from the winch, Sam jumped inside the cab of the water bowser, Tiny and I climbed in the back of the ration Bedford. We joined back with the rest of the Artillery and moved off with the sonorous and blaring sounds of tank fire all round us. It definitely started to feel like war now with all the loud explosions, gunfire and resonant noisiness around us. I sprawled myself all over the kit in the back of the ration Bedford gazing out at the bright stars in the clear sky just thinking of life.

"Shit!" I screamed at the top of my voice.

Whacky races as we go through Iraq. The first one to Kuwait wins!

"What's up, Scouse?" Tiny asked.

"I've just gone and left the fucking gene and me travel bag with some of me uniform in the 1-Tonnie," I replied.

Tiny started pissing himself with laughter because there was nothing I could do about it now. I just hoped I didn't get billed for loss of kit after the war. The British Army is renowned for doing this as I remembered years ago hearing about lads in the Falklands War in 1982, who were killed, and after that conflict when the army realized that they were missing army kit they tried to bill their families to replace it. It was on the news and in the national papers. If it did happen, I'll tell them that I was ordered to leave it all behind; plus, I've got kit insurance anyway. I felt very tired now and drifted of to sleep, thinking of Paula.

I heard extremely loud thundering booms, uproarious explosions and was startled awake from my deep sleep. "What the fuck is that?" I shouted to Tiny has I peered around the side of the ration Bedford.

What I saw was brilliant, and I climbed out of the back of the ration Bedford to have a better look. Looming in the distance and all round was war; to my right about a mile away I saw what I believed to be the explosions of our artillery shells hitting and blowing their targets up. And to my left was that familiar shrill whooshing noise from the night before, which was the sound of the MLRS firing its rockets at the enemy. They

American M109 howitzer and M-2 Bradley infantry fighting vehicle.

were weakening the Iraqi defences, so the infantry could go in and mop up. I watched for about ten minutes before returning back to the back of the ration Bedford to catch up on some needed sleep. The deafening earsplitting noise of the night's battle was murmuring and getting dimmer and dimmer as I drifted back into my deep sleep. When I woke in the morning, we were static, and I noticed that we were no longer with 40-Field Regiment, Royal Artillery, but an element of 21 Royal Engineer Regiment instead. I could tell it was the Engineer's by their units flags attached to some of the vehicles antennas. How we managed to get with 21 Royal Engineer Regiment I didn't know.

There were five or six packets made out of both tracked and wheeled vehicles. Staff Large came round and directly told us all, "Stand to."

That meant we had to be prepared for an enemy attack.

A squaddie from the Engineers came along our packet and told us to dig shell scrapes.

"If you got any anti tank weapons with you, have them to hand, alright?" he added.

"What do we need the anti tank weapons for," I asked him.

"A load of Iraqi tanks are on the loose, and we believe they are coming this way," he informed us.

I had lost my cowardly attitude after seeing the previous night's battle, and I thought this was great and hoped we would see some action. I grabbed the shovel and dug my shell scrape in record time. Once it was completed, I dove in and pointed my Gat in the direction I believed the Iraqi tanks might attack. I didn't set my sights, but left them on the battle sight, which was already set at three hundred meters. I continued to look through them in the hope that a tank would come in the middle. If a tank had come within my Gat's sight, my Gat wouldn't have been much use against a tank, but I sought out any kind of action. We were there for about an hour, and nothing came. Again, I was well pissed off because I thought I would get my first kill. Once it had been established that there was no enemy threat, everyone was ordered to stand down and mount up ready to move.

So, I jumped in the cab of the ration Bedford with Jay and Hutch to be their air sentry. I opened the hatch in the roof of the cab and stood up with my Gat. It was hurting my legs a bit with standing for ages, but I kept a firm grip on my Gat with my index finger of my right hand on the trigger just in case we were going to be attacked by Iraqi aircraft. I sought out any ways of war. However, there wasn't anything I could do with a SLR against a Russian made MiG. Even though the odds were stacked heavily against me, I was still keen enough to stay air sentry. We drove straight into a vicious sandstorm, so I pulled my ski goggles down from my helmet to protect my eyes and placed my sweat rag around my nose and mouth. Trying to see in this storm was unreal, so at the odd moment I would duck down back inside the cab for five minutes to get out of the storm.

We continued through the storm for a few hours before we stopped again. I could see there were two 436-armoured Radio Relay wagons by where we had stopped. I told Staff Large about the Relay wagons, and he went off to try and see if they had comms with anyone to let our Node know that we were fine and whom we were with. Our Node was somewhere behind us I think or if worse, they had been wiped out. There was still plenty of gunfire going on in the distance, but it wasn't as loud as the night before, which must mean we were further back. Staff Large returned after about twenty minutes and informed us that the relays were packing up and had no comms shots in, but would pass on our message once they were set up in their new location.

We were informed that we would be staying in this location over night, because of this; we grabbed the shovels again and got to work on our

Heavy sand storm during the invasion of Iraq.

shell scrapes. Then, we sat around talking about the last couple of days and the lads back in our Node, as there was nothing else for us to do. The night sky was closing in on us as I went for a shovel recce, the MREs wouldn't stay in your system for long. We were living on MREs at the moment, as there wasn't time for us to cook anything. God only knew what the lads back in the Node were living on as we had all the Nodes rations with us. As it become night time, the noise of the surrounding battles grew louder in the desert night's thin air.

36

The battles at night were much better because they sounded a lot closer to us than the sounds actually were. To our right the sky's horizon was flashing with orange glows of tank fire coming from that direction. It was hard to say how far we were from that particular firefight. There were also MLRS being launched to our left. All of this firefighting and lighting of the night sky was remarkably brilliant, making the adrenaline race around my body. I wanted to be in the thick of it all. A sapper came up to our wagons to find out if we were the signal lads that he had heard were tagging along with them. "Can one of your lads come and have a look at my radios?" he asked Staff Large.

I tried to sneak away because I knew with being a Rad Op I would be dicked for being the only one here. "Where's Molloy?" Staff Large called out.

"Here, Staff!" I answered from around the back of the ration Bedford.

"Go along with this lad and see if you can sort out his radios for him," Staff Large ordered.

I went along with the sapper to his wagon, hoping that a newly trained and still wet behind the ears Rad Op could fix his radio sets. Even though I was a qualified B3 standard Rad Op, I hadn't had any real experience with radio installation or fault finding, so found this task a bit daunting. I hadn't been on a proper comms exercise on the magnitude of anything that was happening out here. I hadn't even had any time to settle into 3 Div properly before being thrust into war. The radios were in the back of their CVRT (*Command Vehicle Radio Tracked*), which was a small armoured tracked vehicle. Only one person at a time fit in the back, so the sapper went round to the driver's seat to tell me his radio set up. I had a look at the way the radios were set up, and he had two 353s VHF sets connected to a RCU (*Remote Control Unit*). A radio operator's headset plugged into the RCU that enables him to listen to two different radio nets at the same time or switch between either net whenever he wanted to transmit without having to change headsets. They had no DMUs (*Digital Master Units*), which meant they had no secure comms; as a result, I changed the leads around and tested the knobs on the RCU to see if that would work. I managed to get comms on one of the sets but not the other one.

British Warrior infantry fighting vehicle.

"I've got comms in yeah set 'B,' but I can't find what's the problem with yeah set 'A.' Yeah going to have to find a radio tech to sort out the problem. Sorry, I can't be of any more assistance to yeah mate," I bluffed him.

The sapper thanked me for getting comms in one set as I left to return back to the Bedford's. When I got back, I informed Staff Large that I got comms in one set, and they need a radio tech. Staff told me that I had to go and guard some Iraqi POWs when they were brought to us.

I was dead excited at this bit of news, and it was the first time I was glad to be dicked for a stag. This would be the first time I saw the enemy face to face. Then, I heard an armoured vehicle approaching off in the distance. The engine's sound was familiar. It was the sound of a Warrior, and it was coming from the direction of the firefight. When the Warrior came into sight, I could see around thirty POWs with one British squaddie, walking alongside with his SA80 rifle, guarding the POWs. They were lead into a mine tape compound, which had been hurriedly set up earlier. A huge tarpaulin sheet that we used to cover vehicles had been given to the POWs to keep the wind off them. They all hugged together to keep warm, and they just sat there talking amongst themselves.

They didn't look like soldiers at all, and we knew through our intelligence that most of them were conscripts, which meant they had

184

American M-60 A3 main battle tank.

been dragged off the streets of where ever they came from and put on the front line. They were in shit state and dressed in ragged uniform. Obviously by the sight of them, they were tired, starving and in a state of shell shock. I thought anybody would be in the same condition of the POWs if they had been shelled to fuck for the last few weeks, but I had no pity for them even in this state. The tarpaulin sheet started to flutter off them in the wind, so I told one of the lads to watch my back as I entered the compound to sort out the sheet.

Aas I got close up to them, I noticed that they still had their jumpers and coats on. I hoped that they were searched properly because we had been instructed a few days previous to strip any prisoners from the waist up. This is because there had been reports of some Iraqis strapping booby traps to themselves, hoping to blow their captives up, and when seeing them fully clothed, I was shitting myself a bit. I had a tight grip on my Gat and was relying on it to save my life if need be. I walked in very wary of my surroundings like a burglar about to rob a house. The index finger of my right hand was tight on the trigger, and I wouldn't think twice of squeezing it if they tried anything. I bent over and reached for the tarpaulin sheet with my left hand and kept my eyes firmly fixed on the POWs.

One of the POWs stood up and started to approach me. My trousers were starting to turn a darker shade of brown as I seen my life flash before my eyes. I swiftly dropped the sheet, stood up straight and abroad, brought my left hand up and placed it on the cocking handle, pointing my Gat towards the Iraqi's head. I thought this is the one that hadn't been searched, and I was going to get it. He sharply raised his hands above his head and started to groan to try and communicate with me. I kept my Gat pointing at him has he pointed to the sheet and bent down to pick it up. I would not relinquish my Gat for anything. The relief that came over me was tremendous, and I jokingly thought I could go and put a clean pair of combats on. He turned and took the tarpaulin sheets back to his mates to try and keep them warm. When I walked past the POWs, I couldn't stop thinking that was a close call. A sapper relieved me, and the firefight was still in full swing. It must have been very close as you could hear the engines of the Challenger tanks and Warriors. I didn't think we would have seen any of this action if we were still with our Node I thought.

37

When I awoke in the morning, I found out that the POWs had been taken from our location to a central location where they would be taken to a bigger and more grand POW camp back in Saudi. Staff Large was being his usual 'jack' self by making sure he had a wash and a shave and ordering the rest of us to pack everything away. None of us had had the pleasure of a wash and a shave this morning, and he was pissing us all off. As we finished packing up, a Chinook troop carrying helicopter landed about a kilometer in front of us. I kept looking in the direction of the Chinook to see the reason for it landing so near to our location, and nothing happened for about five minutes until the tail ramp came down. Droves of POWs started to run up the ramp and into the belly of the Chinook. As soon as it was full, it took off to take the POWs to their new home in Saudi for the duration of the war. I could see that there were still plenty of POWs sitting on the desert floor waiting for their 'taxi.' Staff Large told us that we all had to attend a brief.

The Engineer's OC addressed us on the past couple of night's activities. He said that everything was going better and faster than anyone had predicted. The Stafford's, Scots Dragoon Guards and the Queens Royal Irish Hussars managed to go through their objectives of 'Copper' and 'Platinum' in a matter of hours each, instead of the predicted few days on each one. He also added that 4 Brigade had also had the same success as our brigade, and both brigades are now heading towards the objective of 'Varsity'. He pointed to the location of Varsity that was on the map of the enemy positions, which was in the middle of Kuwait, and, then, he pointed to another objective called 'Cobalt' where our brigade would take out the enemy and that would be the end and finality of the war for us. This objective was North West of Kuwait City. We were dismissed back to our vehicles to wait to move. After that brief, I got the impression that it was a race between the two brigades of who could get the most battle honours.

We knew it would be a long day because we would be driving for the best part of it. As we were travelling forward, all the packets had to stop. We stopped at the edge of an Iraqi mine field, and even though it wasn't labelled with signs, as laid down by the Geneva Convention, we could still tell it was a minefield from our pre-Gulf training. There were so-

SPAM Chinook helicopters with loads heading north.

called metal pickets with the odd single strand of barbwire between them. This 'barrier' wasn't completely around the minefield. This particular minefield was an anti personnel minefield, and we were able to tell this by the size of the small depressions in the sand where the mines were buried. The armoured tracked vehicles went first followed by the wheeled vehicles that were trying to stay on the tracks made in the sand by the tracked vehicles ahead. I was watching Hutch from the rear of the ration Bedford driving the water bowser behind us, and he varied off the tracks slightly just missing a mine by about an inch. I covered my ears with my hands to anticipate the sound of the mine going off, but it didn't; moreover, we drove through another minefield a bit further on too.

Another British unit drove past us from another direction and seemed to be going in the direction where we had just come from. Tiny and I watched the driver of a British Army JCB digger stop and jump out. He bent down at the side of his JCB and picked up an Iraqi AK47 assault rifle. Then, he climbed back up into the cab of the JCB clutching his spoil or as we have nicked named them 'Gizits' (*give us it*).

"The fucking jammie bastard!" I screamed out to Tiny.

I've been keeping my eye out for an AK47 to take back home with me as my trophy from this war. The one that had just been picked up was only a couple of hundred yards away. I'd have to keep my eyes even sharper if I want the main prize.

After about another hour's drive, I noticed two Iraqi squaddies running from out of the desert to try and catch our packets, and I pointed them out to Tiny. They didn't have a white flag with them, nor did they have any weapons that I could see. I didn't even consider raising my Gat and trying to shoot them. I suppose I should have though. I think it was the novelty of seeing loose enemy running about for me not raising my Gat and taking a shot at them. They could have had bombs strapped to their chests or any kind of malignant device, and I let them catch our wagons up. Nothing happened to our wagons, so they must have been giving themselves up. Whether the wagons at the rear of our packets had accepted their surrender or not, I didn't know. It was around four o'clock in the afternoon before we stopped again for the night.

We were given another briefing by the Engineer's OC, but this time he told us we were now off to Basra, which is Iraqi's southern most major city, and our job was to take out the Iraqi Republican Guard. Everything else was put on hold for the time being. We would be staying in this location for the night just in case the SPAMs in their bombers got trigger-happy and mistook us for the enemy. Apparently, any movement on the ground at night the SPAMs had been blowing up we were informed at the briefing. Staff Large came over and told us to unpack all the cooking equipment again and set it up for a main breakfast because the Engineers officers wanted a cooked meal in the morning. The six of us just stared with bewilderment as none of us were pleased with Staff Large over setting up the cooking equipment, for we all believed that he went up to the officers, trying to gain brownie points and volunteered our services. How else would the Engineer officers have known that we had a full field kitchen with us? It's alright for him to say that we would do things because it wouldn't be him getting his hands dirty helping us out with the work he had put our way. While we were setting up the kitchen for tomorrow, Staff Large stood there with a steaming bowl of hot water having a wash and shave. I stopped what I was doing and shook my head in disgust with Staff Large's behaviour. What a fucking twat he was, and he certainly knew how to piss us off. Once I had done my share of work, I went to stag on. Nothing happened during the stag and when my two hours was up I headed straight for my doss bag.

I was woken up at three o'clock in the morning and was told to be ready

Iraqi soldiers surrendering.

to move at seven o'clock in the morning. The officers had now decided that they didn't want the cooked breakfast, and we were well pissed off, packing all the kitchen stuff away. Today was Thursday the 28th of February 1991, payday. I should have around thirteen hundred pounds in my account if my mathematics was on the ball. We were given another brief by the Engineer's OC informing us all that a cease-fire was on. I was inquietude and well pissed off now because I wouldn't get the chance to kill an Iraqi. I know it sounds a bit disturbing and horrific, and I'm not trying to be macho, however, I honestly wanted to shoot someone to prove to myself that I could actually kill another human being. Everyone else was made up that it might all be over in a few days. We all jumped in our wagons after one of the officers made a joke about us not leaving any litter about because the Iraqi's were complaining about the mess we are causing to their country. We headed back on our original course to Kuwait and to hope we could at long last meet up with our Node.

On our way to Kuwait, we saw plenty of burnt out Iraqi T55 tanks that were casualties from the previous couple of nights fighting. I even saw my first dead bodies that the SPAMs had forgotten to mop up. This gave me a great opportunity to get my camera and take some more photos. We drove past four Iraqis trying to surrender to us. Two of them were waving

They still want to surrender but we drove straight past them.

bits of white cloth as flags. I reached for my camera again to capture this unique moment in my short war, which was not what I thought it would be. We didn't stop to pick them up, and I thought they were given some food by other passing wagons closer to them until our rear logistic units would take them on board. There had been stories reaching us that lads from other units were tossing the Iraqis tins of food from their ration packs. They gave the Iraqis the tins of powdered milk, sugar, processed cheese and any other crap that they didn't want minus the tin openers to go with them, and the Iraqis relished whatever was given to them. Well, at least they weren't left without any food, even though they couldn't get into the tins to eat the food. Nevertheless, we drove-on to our destination, and, finally, we left Iraq and entered the sovereignty of the Kuwaiti desert in the early evening, as the sun was setting down into the sandy desert.

We came out of the desert and pulled onto a dual carriageway - which we later learnt was the infamous 'Basra road.' A Challenger tank from the Queen's Royal Irish Hussars was static across the carriageway in order to help guard us and make sure we went the right way. When I got to the other side and saw the tank, I couldn't believe my eyes with what they had flying from one of their antennas. They had a big 'William of Orange' flag flying proudly, which stood out like a prostitute in a

An Iraqi T55 tank totally taken out.

convent. There were loads of cars that had been abandoned by the Iraqis trying to escape out of Kuwait, and, also there were clothes strewn all across the carriageway; it was a shit hole. Has we were driving along the carriageway, the wagons had to steer around craters in the tarmac that had been created by our bombers trying to stop the mass exodus of the Iraqi Army out of Kuwait. We stayed on the carriageway for about a mile, dodging craters and burnt out and blown up Iraqi military vehicles. There were British squaddies looking inside all the vehicles and taking things as souvenirs. Yet again, I grabbed my camera and took photographic evidence before turning off the carriageway and all the wagons were parked up about a couple of hundred metres away in all round defence.

38

Once our wagons were parked up in position, Sandy and I got under way, this time, digging a two-man shell scrape, just in case the cease fire broke and in the unlikely event of the Iraqis turning onto the offensive. Staff Large went off to find anybody of officer rank, and, who knew what was happening especially with us. Nevertheless, before he went, he told us to start unloading all the kitchen equipment to make a meal for everyone. We were all pissed off again and slagged him off something rotten for trying to kiss arse and get himself recommended for a MBE (*Member, The Most Excellent Order of the British Empire*) medal.

We nearly had the field kitchen set up when Staff Large returned about fifteen minutes later, walking right in and saying, "Right lads! We are going to move from here to just down the road to where the Iraqis had taken over a Kuwaiti Army camp. When we get there, we will be feeding two hundred Iraqi POWs. So, let's pack everything away," informing us.

"I wandered who fucking dicked us for that job," I said sarcastically to Sandy.

Once we were packed up, we were escorted by a couple of Engineers in their 110 Land Rover to the Kuwaiti Army camp. The abandoned Kuwaiti Army camp was going to be used by the British Army to process

British soldiers looking for souvenirs on the Basra road.

all the Iraqi POWs and we would later that evening be joined in the camp by more British squaddies. When we reached the camp, it wasn't anything like our barracks back home or even our barracks in Germany. The place hadn't been bombed; it was just extremely run down with plenty of trees and bushes growing. A Sergeant Major would have been in his elements with a troop of men in this place, giving it a good 'Area Cleaning' by picking all the litter up and sweeping the sand off the desert floor. When the Iraqis were pulling out of Kuwait, they trashed everything in sight. Those scruffy looking smelly Iraqis probably lived like that even when they occupied the structures as a home; in particular, our camps were better looked after.

Our two Bedford's were parked on the dry concrete floor in the back of our camp undercover of corrugated sheeting - this area turned into our kitchen. Once the kitchen area was up and running it was dark, so I took it upon myself to have a look around the camp to see what I could liberate for myself. It wasn't a big camp, but it had enough buildings of different sizes for me to find something in. I would take my time to investigate each particular building as I didn't want to be missing for too long to arouse any suspicion. In a building next to where we had set up, it was two storeys high with a few windows and a flat roof, which I found it to be nearly pitch black and difficult to see. When I entered the building through the door way I noticed a very dark room to my left. I entered the room with caution for the fear of the room being booby trapped. My right hand was stretched right out in front me searching up and down for possible trip wires that could set off a booby trap and my Gat was in my left hand. As I was clearing the dark room I knocked into a table with my right leg and the table made a little screech as it moved across the floor. I manoeuvred my body around the table going further into the room when I kicked a hollow sounding object with my left foot that was on the ground. I squatted down and reached out with my right hand searching for the object. I took a couple of steps forward before my right hand knocked the object that I had just kicked. Placing my Gat under my left arm, I picked the object up and inspected it with my hands. It was not that hard to make out what the object was with its dome shape and a chin strip for what I had kicked was an Iraqi helmet. At this point I was ecstatic with my find, so I decided to leave the building and when I went outside in the not much lighter environment and found that the helmet was in the same style as the old American World War II helmet. I was made up with myself with this find and raced back to the lads to gloat.

"Look what I've got, lads," I said to them as I pulled the helmet from around my back.

They called me all the bastards under the sun, so I told them not to worry, and that I would go off and try and find more kit for all of us. I went off searching through all the other buildings on the other side of the camp, but this time with my torch. These buildings were single storey that had doors that lead into their own individual rooms, and I was having no luck with it being hard to see with a dim lighted torch as the batteries were running out of power. I was about to call off my search on the last building when I stumbled on what must have been the Iraqis QM's clothing stores. All kinds of clothing filled the store, from boots to Parker's. Indeed, I took enough Iraqi Parkas, helmets, uniforms and other bits and bobs for all seven of us. When I returned back to our kitchen, they were all made up, and I was back on their Christmas card lists.

"Where the fuck did yeah get all that Scouse? The uniforms are still in their plastic bags," Sam said in astonishment.

"There's a whole QM's clothing store over there in one of the buildings," I told them.

Jay wanted to know more, so I took him to where I acquired the gizits. As we got to the door of the clothing stores, another British squaddie who was on guard challenged us. We ran off back to our Bedford's not to be caught. They wouldn't have been able to recognise who we were in the dark.

When we returned, Hutch was cooking up a stew for the POW's. There were all kinds in it from our ten men ration packs and fresh rations like tinned stewing steak, carrots, peas and potatoes, and it smelt nice. When the stew was ready, it was poured into two Norwegian containers for Jay and me to take round to where the POWs were being documented and kept.

In the building, the POWs were separated in three different rooms according to their rank. They all looked very tired, hungry and scared as they were marshalled to their appointed room. They were all given white plastic plates and had to form an orderly line with the junior ranks being fed first. The senior ranks and officers kept on popping their heads out of their rooms. We could see that they weren't happy over this order of feeding. A Sergeant from the Engineers kept on telling them to get back into their rooms and wait their turn. As the POWs came up to get their meal, we could see the starvation on their faces; also, the ages varied from one young lad I saw, who couldn't have been much older than fourteen, and an old man who was in his fifties. There was even another old man who just collapsed and was carried out on a stretcher. The Engineers Sergeant stood by Jay and me as we dished out the food to ensure there was some sort of order. An Iraqi officer kept on coming out of his room and talking to the Engineer Sergeant, "Don't worry. It's all right. Your boyfriend will be here in a minute." The Engineer Sergeant reassured him.

Later, we saw two Iraqi officers walking down the corridor holding hands. "Dirty bent bastards," I said to Jay in disgust on seeing this.

Then, we couldn't stop laughing for ages. Apparently, they were all into fucking each other up the arse. They did that because it had something to do with their Muslim religion - something about their saviour being born man of man the Engineer Sergeant told us. Since it was biologically impossible for this to happen, I thought they were just thick or they just loved getting it up the rear.

It was very late when we finished feeding them, and we left the containers by the Bedford and went straight to bed. It had been a very eventful long day.

When I woke in the morning, it was very early with having to get the breakfast ready for the POW's. Before I started any work, I took this opportunity to have a decent wash with living in my NBC suit for the past week. I peeled off my Everton F.C. boxer shorts, which by now had changed colour from white to grey. My socks could have probably walked off by themselves. There hadn't been the time to change any of my clothes at all during the last week. Instead of putting them in my dobhi bag, I dug a hole in the middle of the camp and buried them. I stood out in the warm morning sun having a good bollock wash, and it felt great letting the fresh desert air swirl around my naked bollocks, which made me feel like a new person afterwards. I put on a brand new set of desert combats that I had been saving for the end of the war. Well, I wanted to look my best in case we had to liberate some city. Sam and I had to take the POWs their breakfast, so we grabbed the metal pot off the cooker, which contained their 'gourmet' meal. Sam knocked the pot into my leg, and it left a large black sticky mark. "Nice one, Sam. You've just dirtied me new kecks," I growled at him.

A Kuwaiti army camp not far from Kuwait City that had been occupied by the Iraqis then by us. This is the camp where we fed and processed the Iraqi PoWs.

Sam just shrugged his shoulders and giggled. The breakfast was another stew, but this time it contained pork sausages, which the eating of pork is forbidden by Muslims. As Sam and I were dishing the breakfast out, an Iraqi Major, who was a doctor, approached us to inspect its ingredients.

"Is there any pork in this food? It is against our religion to eat pork," he asked us curiously.

"No mate, there isn't any thing like that in it," I told him lying through my teeth.

As he turned away, Sam and I looked at one another and said how cheeky he was for asking.

We had heard through the lads taking the POW's details that the Iraqis would wait in their trenches till the British came along before giving themselves up. Apparently, we were the most humane army when it came to the treatment of POWs. But, all this about eating pork was the bullshit of their religion. Every POW that ate their meal was coming for seconds. They were that hungry that if there were a pig on a spit roast, they would have all tucked in. Once we finished feeding the POWs, we could go and have our meal. And on the way back, we noticed a Node outside the camp. I told Tiny about the Node when I got back to our Bedford's, and he went over to their Node Command to try and reach our own Node.

39

Tiny came back after about a half an hour and told us that he was able to get through to our Node, which was still in Iraq, and that Sergeant Clay was coming to fetch us. He also told us that they had put us down as MIA (*Missing in Action*). It was great to know they had faith in us. Jay and I went on a 'Stig' around some more buildings in the camp to find some more gizits. We called it a Stig from the children's television series, 'Stig of the dump,' where a caveman collect all kinds of shit. We found plenty of AK47 magazines and rounds, but no actual AK47 rifles, which was quite disappointing. Jay found some Iraqi propaganda in a desk, which he kept as a souvenir, and I found in the same desk what I believed to be a set of Iraqi soldier's dog tags, as the writing was in Arabic. Holding the Iraqi dog tags in my right hand whilst walking away to go back, I laughed to myself with the thought of some of the bullshit war stories I could come out with to my mates when I got home on how I came in possession of them.

When we returned to the Bedfords, Hutch was preparing to cook the dinner for the POWs. All the Engineer lads thought we were all from the Army Catering Corps. They got a shock when we told them that there was only one 'Sloppy,' and the rest of us were 'Scaley Backs.' I didn't have to feed the POWs after that announcement. When Jay and I had eaten, I decided to fully check out the two storey building opposite our Bedfords, which was the building that I found the Iraqi helmet. I had to climb a couple flights of stairs to get to the main rooms. There were a few small rooms with one large room. There was nothing in the small rooms that was worth nicking, just a few chairs and desks. In the large room, there were maps all over the tables and floors. On the maps were what looked like enemy troop positions, and their advancement movements? They were of no use to us now with a cease-fire in place and the war being effectively over. There were other British squaddies in the building also pillaging the remaining contents. I was told that nothing was to be taken out of the room I was in, and it was to be left for the Intelligent Corps to look at. I was pissed off at this, so I headed back to our Bedfords. When I got out of the building, there was a Jock from the KOSB's (*King's Own Scottish Borderers*) trying to boot one of the doors down. He was ordered to stop by one of his superiors. That was typical infantry mentality, brawn instead of brain. Staff Large informed us that we were packing up because the Jocks were taking over the camp, and they had their own slop jockeys. We moved outside the camp and parked up next to the Node outside to wait for Sergeant Clay.

We had our tea with the lad's from that Node, and it made a change from us slaving away over the cookers. Their set up was very much the same as ours with a TV and video player in the admin tent, and also hanging proudly at the back of the tent was a pig board. I noticed a familiar face from when I joined the juniors. He was in the same troop as my mate Jay Craine. I went over and introduced myself to see if he would recognise me. It took him a while, but he twigged, and we had a laugh reminiscing on our junior days. He told me that they were packing up tonight and moving on to Kuwait City. Their Central, which is the Data Comms wagon, was staying behind. It was dark when the Node moved off, and I tried to get some sleep in the cab of one of our Bedfords, but I couldn't settle. I was freezing.

I woke up at two o'clock in the morning freezing my bollocks off. I couldn't get warm, so I decided to go and sit in the back of the Central where I knew it would be warm. When I walked in the back of the Central, I noticed that Wilkies brother was on shift. We chattered for about an hour and a half about our experiences over the last week. After our conversation I started to feel tired again, so I went back in the cab of our Bedford and managed to grab a couple of more hours of broken sleep.

After, I had got myself washed and dressed and went off on a stig. It was flat dessert for as far as the eye could see except for the odd bump. I came across a few Iraqi bunkers that could have had already been cleared by allied forces, as there tracks in the sand made by wheeled and tracked vehicles, which came in from the direction of the Iraqi border. There were two beds inside the bunker, which was about seven foot long by about six foot wide, and I could tell that the occupants had left in a hurry because there was all clothes strewn all over the bunker. I decided to walk back totally dejected with not finding anything in any of the bunkers. On the way back to our Bedfords, I stumbled onto a few wooden boxes that were on their own on the desert floor. I took the lid off of some of the boxes to see what was inside; some of the boxes contained the artillery rounds, and other boxes contained the cases. I had at long last found something, which would be worth having, and there

An Iraqi Army cap badge found in an Iraqi Army bunker.

were plenty of them. I emptied the sacking of cordite charges from out of one of the cases, so I could take it back with me. The shell cases were made from brass and were of Russian origin. I could tell this because there was Russian writing on them. The bunkers I had just searched must have belonged to an Iraqi artillery battery. I knew that the brass case would look brilliant back at my room in Soest all polished up. The lads would be made up with these, and there was well enough here for our whole Node. I picked one up and placed it under my arm and headed back to the lads.

When I returned, the lads were busy doing nothing.

"Alright lads, see what I've found out in the desert," I shouted.

"Where the fuck did you find that, Scouse?" Jay said in a remarkable tone.

"I've just been on a stig over that way," I replied whilst reaching out my arm and pointing behind me in the direction where I had just walked.

"Is there any more out there, Scouse?" Staff Large asked me.

I stood there in shock with Staff Large calling me 'Scouse'; he usually referred to me as 'Molloy' to keep it all formal, so he must be after something I thought.

"There is a fucking shit load out there. Boxes of the stuff," I told him.

Staff Large told us all to jump in a Bedford and go out on a stig, and he would stay behind and watch the rest of the kit. The remaining six of us jumped in the ration Bedford and headed in the direction of where I found the artillery cases. We picked enough cases up for all seven of us before we set off in a different direction, driving for about a further ten minutes out into the desert before we came across another artillery location. We de-bussed from our Bedford, and it was every man for himself; as we all darted off in different directions to pillage the bunkers for gizits. There was nothing to find in these bunkers as well except for old clothes and beds. The Iraqis that were in this location had left in a hurry, and we could tell that this place hadn't been searched or even attacked during the war because none of the wheeled or tracked vehicle tracks that I had seen at the previous location were at this location. There was nothing in the bunkers worth having, so Sam and I went playing around on an Iraqi AA (*Anti-Aircraft*) gun that had been abandoned. I was on the wheel for elevation of the AA gun barrel, and Sam was on the wheel for directing the AA gun.

"Bandits ten o'clock high. Boom, boom, ba-boom," I screamed out whilst looking through the sights and elevating the barrel.

We had a laugh messing about on the AA gun until we jumped off it and the breach opened, and surprisingly there was a live round still in it. We shit ourselves on seeing that the gun was loaded. We could have had a nasty accident if we would have pressed the trigger. Jay came out of a bunker waving a black Iraqi beret in his hand. At least one of us found something. Once we searched the immediate area, which had been fruitless for most of us, we all jumped back inside the Bedford to search out more bunkers. We came across another artillery location about five minutes later further out in the desert towards Iraq. The bunkers in this location were constructed better than the last ones. They were in a triangular formation with a trench connecting each bunker. This location could have possibly been their RHQ. In one of the bunkers, I came across a wooden box that was tightly secured with a padlock, but it didn't take me long to smash the padlock off. Inside was a few papers that was of no use or interest and personnel stuff of its owner. The only thing worth salvaging in the box was what looked like a homemade Iraqi flag, which could have been made for a loved one as he went off to war. It was the best gizit I had managed to get my hands on yet. I also found an Iraqi laser range finder, which was still boxed and still worked and the instructions were in English. The laser range finder was painted with desert colour paint with grey painted patches and would be mounted on a tripod. There was also a battery charger that accompanied it. I couldn't manage to take it back with me, so Tiny claimed it and took it has his.

"Look what I've got," shouted Jay with excitement.

The lucky bastard found an Iraqi bayonet from an AK47 assault rifle. Indeed, that was definitely the find of the day. This site was a lot more fruitful and as soon as we got has much as we could carry, we made our

Blown up Iraqi Anti-Aircraft gun just inside Iraq.

way back to our location.

When we got back this time, we unloaded all the gizits and set them all up on and around a table for a photo with all seven of us standing behind everything. We gave the lads from the Central our cameras to do the honours of taking photographs. From that moment on we called ourselves the 'Desert Stigs.' We'd been out all day, and after tea we decided to go back out on another stig. This time we went even further out into the desert before we reached a fresh location. Same again with this location - it had not been reached by Allied Forces. We couldn't see much inside the bunkers with the night sky promptly starting to draw in on us, and just as we were about to give up hope of finding something, we stumbled across a safe.

Jay and I looked at each other with big smiles on our faces as it felt as if we had won the Pools. The safe was about 2ft x 2ft x 3ft and was locked solid. We heard stories from the Engineer lads in the abandoned Kuwaiti Army camp of squaddies coming across safes, and of the safes being full of Kuwaiti money and gold. I didn't know how true these stories were, but it made me even more eager to get the safe open. The safe was locked, and we tried every thing we could to get it open. I went and got a pick and started to strike the underneath of the safe with it. I managed to split a bit of the weld; nonetheless, I still couldn't get into the safe. Jay tried and came out with the same result.

"Fuck this Jay. I'll go and get one of me grenades and take it outside and grenade the fucker," I screamed furiously.

As we got the safe out of the bunker, Staff Large and Sergeant Clay turned up in a Land Rover. "Come on lads! We're off to join the rest of the Node," Staff Large shouted to us.

"Staff, we've found a fucking safe here, and it's locked. There could be loads of money or gold in it. I've got to try and get the fucking twat open," I told them.

"Just leave it where it is Molloy. We're going now," Staff Large ordered.

Jay and I were both pissed off with having to leave the safe behind in the middle of the Kuwaiti desert. We will never know what was in that safe, and Staff Large could have least let us take it with us, the twat. My morale had taken a mesmerized nosedive with leaving the safe behind, and I remained quiet for the rest of the journey to our Node.

The 'Missing in Action' seven that was left behind by our troop when we crossed the breach into Iraq and ended up just outside Kuwait City when our troop was back in Iraq.

40

When we finally arrived back in our Node, there was plenty of mail waiting for me. They were all mainly from Paula, and she kept on going on about having a baby when I came home. She was doing my head in with all these letters on having a baby. I was chosen to stag on and pan bash as soon as I entered our new location, which was typical. They probably thought we were skiving for the last week. It was really shit being back in the node with all the fucking bullshit.

I went and tracked Flinnie down, and when I found him, I found out that the lucky bastard had managed to get his hands on an AK47 assault rifle. I was jealous of him for having the main prize, the prize I desperately wanted and now with the war over that prize would be out of my grasp. With my sulking face I went to stag on and to get over my disappointment.

After my stag, I went and found Jay and Flinnie and the both of them were playing cards in Flinnie's tent. In between playing cards all-night and discussing each other's views on the war, I managed to find the time to write blueys to Paula, my mother and a mate, Ian Collins, from my estate in Liverpool.

There wasn't much for me to do today except sunbathe, so I grabbed my camp cot and placed it outside my tent. I had to catch up with rudely being interrupted with a little war we just had, but this would be it now, back to the old routine prior to the invasion. I've noticed that my body was starting to go brown, and my legs were still as white as snow. This is the first time I'd ever gone any shade of brown, with having ginger hair and fair skin. However, there should be plenty of time to change that before returning back to Germany. As I was lying in the afternoon sun, Jim and Lieutenant Naden came back from being out on a stig. They had loads of goodies with them. They had about six AK47 assault rifles. "Is there any chance of having one of those AK's, sir?" I eagerly asked Lieutenant Naden.

"I'm going to see if any of the Sergeants want any of them first and if there's anything left, we'll see," he replied as he brushed past me and headed straight for Node Command.

It's always the same; they look after themselves and don't give a toss about the lads. On the contrary, Jim approached me and dragged me by

My Iraqi AK47 Assault Rifle bayonet which Jim gave me
and the RAF Police didn't find.

my arm into our tent and showed me what he had managed to evade from Lieutenant Naden. I entered our tent being lead by Jim and when I pulled the flaps of the tent back, Jim reached for his doss bag. He pulled his sleeping bag back to reveal six AK47 assault rifle bayonets; indeed, it was very enlightening to see what had been omitted from Lieutenant Naden. "Very nice," I said with a wide smile and continued, "Is there any chance of yeah giving us one of them?" I asked with excitement.

Jim reached down, picked one up and gave one to me. I was made up to bits with it because it went well with the rest of my collection.

I would sell most of my gizits, like the Iraqi uniform, when I get home. I know of a shop in Liverpool called 'Liverpool Militeria' by the Birkenhead tunnel that deals in uniforms and other military memorabilia. I used to buy my British Army cap badges from that shop when I collected them during my time back in the ACF. After I thanked Jim and packed my AK47 bayonet. I manoeuvred my way over and had a word with Wilkie to let him know that I bumped into his brother back in Kuwait. Seemingly, everything was winding down with the war, and my mental state had turned more towards getting out of the desert and this ordinance and back home.

I received a bluey from my mates, Mick and Shelly, letting me know how things were back home. So, I wrote back to them and let them know that I got through the war unscathed, and that I couldn't wait to get back to Germany to start my leave.

The weather was really shite the next day. First, it was thundering and lightning. Then, it started to pour down with rain, and our entire location was flooded out; therefore, I decided that I would stay in my tent and only venture outside for the meals and the three times I was staging on today. The only highlight of the day, if it could be classed as a highlight, was the visit to our location of the SSM and the squadron OC. They never came round and spoke to any of us, not that we wanted them to do anyway. I wrote a few more blueys to Paula and members of my family before getting my head down for an early night.

It was a new day, and a Major entered our location. None of the lads were informed way this Major was in our location. I didn't have a clue to whom he was or what unit he was from - not that I gave a shit - it was just a ball ache for the lads in respect that we had to hide all our gizits and the British Army motorbike which the Node had found during their travels last week from Saudi into Iraq. The reason why we had to hide the motorbike was only because the Major knew that our Node would not be issued with one as it is not an operational requirement for a Node to be in possession of a motorbike and too many awkward questions would have arisen. The Major remained for the most of his time in Node Command and I decided I wanted to entertain myself.

The sun decided to appear itself today, so Jay and I grabbed the football and had a little kick around for a bit. And once the Major left our location, Sergeant Clay brought the motorbike back out, and we all had a cabbie on it. I wasn't all that impressed with the bike because I couldn't ride one to save my life.

When the mail came in today, I got a couple of blueys from Paula. I knew what the contents would be before I even opened them. I was right; she wanted a baby. It pissed me off, so I wrote back to her and told her to shove having a baby, and that I wasn't interested.

In the morning we were ordered to pack up our location because we were moving back to Al Jubayl until we were going home. How long that would be, no one could tell us. Hastily, it didn't take us long to pack up, and we formed one long packet waiting for our permission to move. Staff Large came down the packet, and we had to hand in all our ammunition and grenades. There should have been one less grenade for me to hand in as I still thought I could have used a grenade on that safe back in Kuwait. As the handing in of munitions was going on, a few SPAM vehicles came by us, and they stopped to talk to us. They were engineers, and they were out blowing up any Iraqi equipment they could find. They asked Daz Kirby if he wanted to blow up an Iraqi fuel pod that was about five minutes away. They got permission from Lieutenant Naden, and off they went.

When Daz returned with the SPAMs he still had the excitement on his face with just blowing up the Iraqi fuel pod. Daz shook the hands of the two SPAMs that brought him back and once he thanked them for his unforgettable experience he climbed into the cab of his Relay Bedford, so we could make the long journey back to Al Jubayl that would take the Node via Kuwait City and down the East coast of Kuwait and Saudi. Being a nice day, I travelled in the back of the water bowser Bedford. We travelled for ages before we had a proper stop, and by this time I managed to climb on top of the canvas canopy of the Bedford and catch some more UVs. Where we stopped, was an old Iraqi location with some burnt out Iraqi T55 tanks, and some that were still unscathed? Dicko got out and went over to have a look around, and he came back with an AK47. When everyone saw what he had found, we all jumped out of our wagons without permission and raced over to see if we could find anything collectively. There was nothing worth having, and there was loads of hand grenades dotted all around, so we had to be careful of what we picked up just in case it had been booby-trapped. As we approached the road that would lead us to Kuwait City, we could see some of the oil wells that the Iraqi's had set on fire. The sky was so dull and smokey that you couldn't really tell what time of day it was - it was nearly dark in the daytime. There were loads of cars on the embankments of either side of the road, and they all had been wrecked. This chain of cars went on for miles, so I grabbed my camera and took a picture of it before getting some sleep.

The sun was shining brightly by the time I woke up the next day. We were well into Saudi, in fact, we were just outside Al Jubayl. I don't recall stopping during the night. I must've been well away. I found it was quite comfortable sleeping on the cam nets. Our new location was on top of quarry that overlooked the port city of Al Jubayl. Jay, Jim and I set up a 12ft x 12ft tent for us to sleep comfortably and once that was up, we went over and helped the slop jockeys set up the kitchen. In addition, mail came in today. The mail service on the whole, whilst we've been out here, had been quite good. I received a letter from a pen pig, and she sounded a right bore. I wrote back to her for a laugh, telling her what had just happened over the past couple of weeks. I wrote a sloppy bluey to Paula to make up for the nasty one I sent her the other day over the baby, and I hope she hadn't finished with me. I needed to get to a phone and call her to explain before she received the nasty bluey. After I had written my bluey's, I decided to try and get my fitness back up to scratch.

I went over to one of the Centrals to use one of the lad's weights. I tried to get back into the swing of things for when I return to Germany. After a strenuous and fitful workout, I went and watched a video in the admin tent for awhile. Staff Large entered the admin tent and he informed the lads that were watching the tele that this would be our final destination for the duration of our tour, which would be over in about a further six weeks. He also informed us that the Army wanted volunteers to stay behind for a further four months when everyone went back home. Even though I was keen to get back home, the thought of having the opportunity to save some more money for my wedding next year was too great to miss out, so I too went over to Node Command and placed my name on the list. When I was returning to the admin tent I noticed that a couple of Bedfords were leaving our location.

A couple of the Central and Relay Bedfords were sent further up the hill behind us, where there were some SPAMs. The reason for this was our Node would be providing the final Ptarmigan link into Al Jubayl for the planned allied forces withdrawal from Saudi. As I settled back into watching the tele, Staff Large came back into the admin tent and ordered me to go in my 1-Tonnie with one of the Central Bedfords and take them to the FMA (*Force Maintenance Area*). I took myself over to my tent to pick up my 1-Tonnie keys and got into my 1-Tonnie and headed with the Central Bedford, out of our location. I had to escort the Central Bedford to the FMA, where the lads would be remaining with their Central Bedford until they would return to Germany. Once the lads had their Central Bedford settled in and were happy, I went to Camp 4 to use the phones.

I bought a phone card from the shop in Camp 4 and when I was in the shop I noticed a poster on the wall advertising a football match, which was being screened this evening in the camp's NAFFI. This match appealed to me because it was Everton versus West Ham United and I had to come back later on to watch the match. When I got to the phone, it took me ages to get through to Paula. It was great to hear her voice again, and I told her that I'd volunteered to stay for four more months to help save money for our wedding. She started to cry and warned me that if I didn't get my name off the list, that it was over between us. I calmed her down and reassured her that once I was back in my location, I would take my name off the list. She was happy with that, and she told me she would be writing me a bluey tonight and explaining in it what she is going to do to me in a sexual nature on my return home. I couldn't wait to go home; I wished I were there with Paula now because Paula had a fantastic slim, olive skinned body. Her tits were small, but that didn't bother me because I was a legman. And when I went down on Paula, I used to love licking the inside of her well-toned thighs. She had perfect legs. We both liked it when I made her cum with my tongue, and I would spend ages pleasuring her in this way. I also loved licking my tongue over her flat firm stomach before reaching her small pert tits. Whilst I used to lick and nibble her shoulders and neck, Paula would grab my hand and place it in her knickers, so I could place my middle finger up inside her tight pussy. I had to stop picturing Paula and me in the heat of passion has I was getting myself too excited and turned on.

When I returned back to our location, I headed straight to Node Command and asked Lieutenant Naden to take my name off the volunteers list and explained the telephone conversation I had with Paula. He was sound about it, and said he would see what he could do as the list had already been sent off. I also asked him if Corporals Gaz Tuff, Mick Duggan and I could go into Camp 4 tonight to watch Everton versus West Ham United. Lieutenant Naden said we could but only if a Sergeant went with us. When I left Node Command I went round and asked all the Sergeants if any of them would come with us to Camp 4, but they all said no. That was it. We were well pissed off, for it was as if we weren't even trusted to go and watch a football match on our own. It was not as if we could have a few pints and start fighting. Strangely, just a couple of weeks ago, we were trusted with hundreds of 7.62mm rounds, grenades and 66's, those dangerous pieces of kit, and yet not trusted to watch a game of football. All the higher-ranks were fucking pricks that needed to grow up.

41

We started to live day to day, for we hadn't had a clue as to what was happening. Therefore, I got as much sun bathing in as possible each day. On one occasion Staff Large started to get all authoritarian - a real knob, which started to piss us all off again. I thought we should have been able to take things a bit easy now until we returned to Germany and the barrack type of soldiering. He informed us that we would all be up at eight o'clock in the morning to start work at nine o'clock. The time wasn't all that bad to me, but it was the guard duties he wanted us to do, and I didn't much care for that. Not one of us could see the point of staging on during the day anymore; furthermore, there wasn't any real work to do. I took a walk to my tent to get away from Staff Large. Shortly after, Lieutenant Naden came into my tent and informed me that he was unable to strike my name off the volunteers' list. I was gutted when he told me that. All I wanted to do now was to get home to Paula and all that sex that I had missed out on over the past few months.

I went off to have a talk with Dave Taylor, who was a Radio Relay Op on Andy's det, and we talked about what we were going to do when we got out of this place. Dave told me that we could get cheap flights through the army to an array of certain places in the world. They are called indulgent flights - flying with the R.A.F. to wherever they flew. It all seemed great; on the other hand, the only problem was that service personnel traveling in this way needed proof of their return fare to fly by a civvy airline because there wasn't always a guaranteed return flight with the R.A.F. Nevertheless, it still put an idea in my head, so I wrote a bluey to Paula and told her that when I get back I would take her to Cyprus for a holiday.

Cyprus is an island in the Mediterranean Sea and a popular holiday destination for Brits seeking a sun soaked holiday. At one time Cypriot Greeks and Cypriot Turks had lived in harmony with each other until a war broke out in 1974 between the two peoples. As a result of this war, Cyprus was now divided in two between the Cypriot Turkish occupied north and the Cypriot Greek occupied south. There is a no mans land - Buffer Zone, between the two boundaries. This Buffer Zone went through the island's capital city, Nicosia, and as a result, Nicosia is the only remaining divided capital city in the world. The country had once been part of the British Empire and as a result Britain still had two Sovereign Base Areas on the island that contained British forces, which are situated in the south. Hopefully, that would cheer her up a bit; after all, we've never had a holiday together. Dave and I chatted for a bit more until dinner, and, then, we both went off to eat. After dinner we played football for the entire afternoon, and it was a great game even though the side I was on got hammered with a loss. After the game, I managed to get a shower before tea. Even though the water was cold, it felt great. No-one really spoke during our tea as they were all probably tired after the game of football. I went straight to my tent after tea to sort out my dobhi for tomorrow. Suddenly, Sergeant Clay entered our tent and informed Jay and me that the both of us were on six hours notice to get ready to go back to Germany. We were both over the moon with this bit of news that we would soon be home. Staff Large had come round to our tent while Jay and I were packing our personal kit and collected our NBC suits from us, as well as all our bits of medical kit like morphine syringe and NAPS tablets. This put us both on a natural high for the rest of the night, and, when Flinnie and Wilkie came round to our tent that evening to play cards, Wilkie was well pissed off when we told him we were leaving.

We received some mail today for the first time in a few days. I received a letter from my mam and a bank statement. The balance of my account was one thousand-three hundred and eighty five pounds, which I was quite happy with, and when this month's wages went in, I had about eighteen hundred pounds. There was no sign of our flight today, so I was dicked to go in the back of the admin Bedford to sort out Staff Large's living arrangements. I was pissed off with doing shit like that to begin with, but shortly, I cheered up, knowing I'd be away from the fat twat in a day or two, although out of nowhere Mick Duggan came over and started to give me loads of verbal abuse because West Ham United beat Everton 2-1.We were all football fans. And once I had turned Staff Larges sleeping arrangements into the Ritz Hotel, I went on a water re-supply with Mark, and on the way back, we popped into Camp 4 to pick Jay Curley up.

It was dark by the time we returned back in our location, and we went straight into the admin tent to see what was happening. The tele was on and the old videos had been played so much that we all knew the words to them, and they were getting boring now. We hadn't had any recent videotapes sent to us for awhile. Flinnie came into the admin tent half pissed. Today was his birthday and he had celebrated it at his parents' house; instead of being stuck in the admin tent, we all headed back to our tent. We left the excitement of the admin tent for the more casual and peaceful atmosphere of our tent. No sooner had we settled down to a card game of 'Sergeant Major', Flinnie reached down into his bag and pulled out a few bottles of booze. "See what I've brought back with us," Flinnie said with a quirky smirk on his face.

Jay and I reached for our mugs and managed to get a bit merry after a few drinks from his dad's home brew. One of the lads came into our tent and told Jay and me that we were going to Camp 4 tomorrow and to get ready to go home.

"Fucking nice one," I shouted out.

I had to take a break from playing cards and having a drink for an hour between midnight and 1 a.m. to do a stag, patrolling the vehicles. I thought this was totally a waste of time, because the war was over, so I went to the toilet for a shit to waste some of the time. When my stag was over, I went to rejoin the party in our tent and had a few more drinks before going to bed.

As soon as I was up, dressed and washed, I packed all my personal kit away. I took my large pack from my 1958 pattern webbing round to the techs, so they could put it on their wagon to take back to Germany for me. I had to leave my camp cot with the Radio Relay lads too. In addition, I had to make my artillery shells safe before leaving them with someone. I placed them upside down with the percussion cap facing up. I placed my left hand over my left ear and grabbed hold of a ball hammer with my right hand. I was shitting myself as I struck the percussion cap with the hammer just in case my hand blew off, despite that nothing happened. By this point I was attracting a small audience and the lads were given me jeers and shouting to me that I would blow myself up. I struck it again and much harder this time. It gave a dull bang, and the shell jumped a couple of feet in the air before landing on its side. The lads started to laugh as they seen me shaking, but I was still in one piece, and it was a relief that it was over and after my successful attempt at bomb disposal, I couldn't understand why I was shitting myself in the beginning.

Sergeant Scott from Trunk Node 063 came to our location to take Jay and me to Camp 4. Once in Camp 4, we tracked down 063 accommodation to have a word with our mates that we hadn't seen for a while. We found them and started to swap war stories with one another. Because Trunk Node 063 was the last Node from our Squadron to cross the breach into Iraq, we told them that they had crossed the breach after the EFI (*Expeditionary Force Institutes*) wagon, which was the NAAFI's support for British forces in the field. Jay and I pissed ourselves laughing, however, for some reason they didn't see the funny side. Well, fancy a bunch of civvies in uniform that sell Mars bars and boot polish entering Iraq before you did! Then, Sergeant Clay told us that there wasn't any room at Camp 4, and that we would have to stay at Blackadder camp, which had taken its name from the BBC's television comedy series, 'Blackadder', and was also known as 'Tent City.' Tent City was in Al Jubayl and used as a transit camp for soldiers waiting to return home after the war and during the war, it was used to accommodate BCRs (*Battle Casualty Replacements*). Notionally, a BCR was to replace those fatalities or wounded soldiers on the battlefield. The camp was given its obvious nickname because it was a camp made entirely from tents. Tent City was about a half mile down the road from Camp 4, and, when we got there, there were a few lads from Trunk Node 043, who were also coming home with us. I took a walk around the camp and found out that the Engineers Post Office was open, so I went and withdrew three hundred Riyals from my savings account to buy a few things.

42

Jay and I decided to take a walk to the EFI tent via the WRAC accommodation, since it was on the way to the EFI, so we could have a blimp at any women that might be loitering there and we saw a little more than what we expected to see. There was a woman sunbathing outside on a camp bed and wearing a bikini. We made it a bit obvious that we were ogling her, but we couldn't help but to look. She was fit as fuck with long blonde hair, and she was very slim, unlike a typical WRAC, who was normally short, podgy with a big fat arse. She noticed us looking at her, and, when she looked right at us, we sharply turned our heads in a different direction and carried on walking to the EFI tent.

As we entered the EFI tent, there were lads waiting patiently in a queue coming from the counter, so Jay and I joined the rear of the queue. We didn't have to wait too long to be served as the queue went down pretty quick. I bought Paula 200 Regal King size cigarettes, my cousin, Andrew, a Gulf War Hard Rock Café T-shirt and myself a shemagh. As Jay was waiting to get served, the blonde Goddess bird that we had just been perving on at the WRAC accommodation walked into the EFI tent. She looked straight at both Jay and I, and we just smiled back at her before she turned her head away. This time she wasn't as viewing and had a green army T-shirt and combats on that were covering her wonderful figure. Even though she was in uniform, she was the only girl that I had seen who wore army uniform nobility well. Jay and I passed comments to each other of what we would like to do to her, and I thought she heard us because she glanced back over at us sharply. Jay and I hurriedly left the EFI tent before she could confront the pair of us. Jay headed back to our tent while I went to see what goods were on sale in the camp's troggy shop.

I had a good look around the troggy shop and the only item I was interested in buying was a camera. The one I had only cost me ten pounds from Argos and was about to pack in on me. To test my new camera, I took a couple of photos of us in Tent City. We had an early night, for we had been informed that a shopping trip was being laid on the following day for a load of us from the camp.

After breakfast the next morning, we all jumped in a Land Rover and went to the Post Office in Camp 4 and got our water money sorted out for the month, but it wasn't open yet. I got to take a shower in 063's block, and, when I came out, I looked white. My suntan must've just been dirty dusting from the desert. However, I felt like a new person afterwards. Once I had gotten out of the shower, Jay and I went to see if the Post Office had opened, and it was, so we both collected over one thousand Riyals each, went for some burgers and chips and a phone card. Luckily, there were quite a few phones free that morning. So, I phoned Paula.

"Hello, Paula?" I asked.

"Yeah, who is it?" she replied in curiosity.

"It's me, Peter. Guess what? I'm coming home tomorrow night. Well, I'm flying back to Germany," I told her.

She was made up and started to cry.

"I'll have to go now love. I'll phone yeah when I get back to Germany. Love yeah."

After I talked to Paula, we went back to Tent City for our dinner.

Even though we ate burgers and chips at Camp 4, it didn't fill us, so we went to the cook house, which was a big tented area away from where we slept. There were R.A.F. slop jockeys as well as army slop jockeys who cooked the food. They had the local troggy's serving the food. The food was quite delicious for the conditions the slop jockeys cooked it in, or it might have been because there was help from the R.A.F. As Jay and I threw away our plates and cutlery in the bins, we noticed a woman walk out of the segregated officer's mess area. She was the fit blonde that we were letching at yesterday. She looked gorgeous in her combats, green T-shirt and her blonde hair tied up in a bun and when she seen us, she gave us an enrapturing cheeky smile as if to say you didn't know I was an officer did you? Jay and I turned and looked at one another with looks of shock and surprise on our faces, and, then, we started to laugh. When she disappeared, we made our way back to our tent to get ready for our shopping trip.

All of us went on the charabanc to the next town of Al Khobar for a shopping spree. We shared the coach with members of the Queens Own Highlanders band, which is a Scottish regiment and whose job, in time of war, were stretcher-bearers. Jay and I sat next to each other and I chatted to a couple of them, who were sitting behind us, on the way to the shops, and they advised us to haggle with the shopkeepers, for they had been out there before and knew the score. I told them that I knew a couple of lads in their battalion from Liverpool who were in the Liverpool Scottish cadets at the same time I was in the cadets. The bandsman told me that they get a few Scousers in their battalion because of the Liverpool Scottish TA and cadets. Nonetheless, once we were dropped off at the shops, Jay and I split from the Jocks.

The first place we went in was a shopping centre with all kinds of different shops. We looked mainly in jewellery shops, but we didn't ask for anything just yet because we didn't have the bottle to haggle at the time. First, Jay plucked up the courage and bought a gold necklace for one hundred and seventy five Riyals. Next, I bought the same necklace for Paula for one hundred and fifty Riyals. All the jewellery was priced in weight, and all the necklaces were all coiled on drums, and the shop assistant pulled off has much gold as we could afford. Then, we went and bought some aftershave from a troggy with a stall in the aisle. I haggled him down on two bottles of Calvin Klein's Obsession perfume for Paula and the aftershave for me. The stall owner spoke very good English and kept going on about Johnnie Holmes, a porno star. I asked him how he knew about Johnnie Holmes when they were not allowed porn movies. He told me that they had ways of getting the stuff over here. We had a bit of a laugh with him before going to buy some T-shirts. There were all kinds of different cartoon type of pictures on the front of the T-shirts depicting the defeat of Iraq. We couldn't haggle over the T-shirts, and they were all the same price of thirty five Riyals, as in the other shops. I noticed one shirt that had a picture of an American A-10 Thunderbolt II tank buster aircraft on it.

"Jay, this T-shirt should say Brit buster not tank buster," I exclaimed to Jay.

He sniggered at the fact of really knowing what the SPAMs did by blowing up one of our Warriors in a blue on blue incident when we invaded Iraq. There was another snigger behind us, and, when we turned around, there was a huge husky black SPAM standing behind us looking at T-shirts too. "What unit are you guys with?" he asked us.

"Were with the first UK armoured division," I proudly replied.

"Yeah, I've heard of you guys. Ya'll did a good job," he praised before leaving the shop.

"Fucking Spams...useless bastards," Jay growled.

Once we had bought a few T-shirts each, we decided to go for a pizza and something to drink. The pizza parlour was in the corner of the shopping centre. Jay and I both ordered a ham and pineapple pizza and a couple glasses of coke. When the pizzas arrived, they were massive, and we only ordered medium ones. Neither one of us could finish the whole pizza. They were very tasty, and we would be full for the rest of the night. As we stood up to leave, we looked out of the pizza shop's window and saw two male troggy's walking down the road holding hands. "Fucking arse bandits," Jay snarled as we left.

We decided to leave the confines of the shopping centre and have a look down the side streets. We went into another jewelry shop that sold all Rolex watches. These watches were far cheaper than back home, but they were still way too expensive for us lowly Signalmen to buy. We found another jeweller, but we didn't have much time to spend in there because they were closing for prayers, so Jay and I purchased the same item again, but this time it was a ring. We got seventy-five Riyals knocked off. I thought we could have gotten more knocked off, but I was still a bit nervous about haggling. I thought if I had been Arthur Daley's prodigy I could have done a lot better. The rings were twenty-one carat gold with a flower on each side and the national emblem of Saudi Arabia on the face. The Saudi Arabian national emblem is of two Sinbad the Sailor type swords with a nicely fit date palm tree above them. There wouldn't be many people back in the UK with those types of rings, for they were a quite unique piece of jewelry. The colour of the gold in Saudi Arabia was a lot darker than the gold back in the UK. On leaving that shop, we made our way back to meet the coach to take us back to camp.

43

There was a buzz on the coach with everyone showing each other what they bought. One of the Jocks bought his wife loads of gold and his kids some toys. "I'll definitely be on a promise when I get back to Germany when I show her all this gold," he told us laughing hysterically. No one was disappointed with what they had bought.

I managed to get a bit of sleep on the coach on the way back. When we arrived back at Tent City, it was late, dark and there were no lights on in our tent, so I had to feel my way to my pit tripping over bits of kit that had been left scattered on the sand floor. I was that tired when I returned that I didn't even attempt to pack away what I had bought; instead, I left them at the side of my Bergen until the morning.

When I woke up, I smiled widely and happily, knowing that this would be my last day in the Gulf. I knew it wouldn't be long before I would get to see Paula again, and that really cheered me up. We finished packing away our last bits of personnel kit, wrapping our Gats in Hessian and getting ready to go directly to the airport. The weather was perfect with the hot sun shining brightly down upon us. Our transport didn't pick us up until the afternoon, so we spent the morning cleaning out the tent, making sure none of us had left any personnel kit or rubbish behind, and as the day went on, we waited, finding these finality of things to do, and, finally, the transport came and took us to the checking in centre, where we would be getting our kit checked by the snowdrops, who were the R.A.F. police. The reason why they are called snowdrops is because the top halves of their peak caps are white.

We were all given a brief on what we were allowed and not allowed to take on the plane with us. A big board hung on the wall behind us showing what contraband was and what they had already confiscated from the other troops. There were numerous amounts, along with different kinds of contraband, such as an AK47 rifle to medical supplies. I had to hand my Iraqi NBC decontamination kit over to the snowdrops because of its medical contents. They even wanted any weapons or parts of weapons like bayonets. "There's no way they're getting hold of me fucking bayonet," I told Jay.

And, then, I unscrupulously repacked my Bergen before I went through customs.

We sat outside under the night sky with the others, who were boarding the coach to leave too, until the snowdrops called us forward formality and searched our kits. I noticed that the curvaceously fit blonde-haired officer was on our flight, and she was also in the Royal Signals. "I wouldn't mind taking her to bed and giving her a good going over." I quietly uttered to Jay.

We started to laugh, but I didn't think she heard us this time. She turned around and smiled at us both. "Oh fuck Scouse. She must've heard yeah," Jay said to me with nervousness in his voice.

"I don't think she did," I said with a reddened face as I started to blush.

The snowdrops called us forward ready for our kit to be searched.

There were a couple of rows of tables with about four snowdrops on each row. There was a bit of a queue at the first snowdrop, so I schematically walked past him and carried on to the end of the table to pretend I was getting my kit searched there. I walked straight past the last snowdrop pretending that I had just had my kit searched by the first snowdrop. I placed my kit straight on the back of the Bedford with all the other searched bits of kit, getting away with my intelligently nimble-witted planned scheme. Once through this point, there was an EFI wagon where we could spend the last of our Riyals before leaving the country. I didn't have much left, so I bought some sweets for the journey back to Germany and some desert rat stickers. The coaches were waiting for us outside, and, when they were full, they left for the airport and then returned for the others. I quickly went to the toilet before jumping on the coach just in case there was no chance of going elsewhere.

When we arrived at Dhahran International airport, there were no chairs for us, so we just lounged on the floor. I took some more pictures of us in the airport to continue my documentation of my experiences. We had been left for about an hour before we were informed that we could board our flight with non-smokers at the front and smokers at the rear. We knew the plane would be full, so we got up straight away to be one of the first on the plane. As we were leaving the building, there was a group of lads, standing not that far from us, with the Blackadder patch on their arm looking at us as if we were shit. We had our war torn desert combats on while they had their nicely pressed desert combats on with the sewn in creases on.

"Cheeky fucking REMF bastards. Who the fuck do they think they're looking at?" Jay said angrily and odiously, so they could hear him.

The REMF's (*Rear Echelon Mother Fuckers*) heard Jay and just turned their heads away obviously embarrassed that they had spent their war safely took away in the rear back in Al Jubayl.

We made the short walk across the tarmac to the waiting Lockheed Tristar R.A.F. passenger plane and climbed the mobile stairs. Once everyone had boarded and sat in their seats, the R.A.F. stewards came round with a small bottle of white wine and a can of Paderborner Pils for every passenger. Everyone was made up to have a drink after so long going with out any beer. The wine was like vinegar, but the lager went down has a treat. The lights came on for us to fasten our seat belts, and the engines started to fire up. Now, everyone got extremely excited with the anticipation of finally going home. The plane started to taxi out to the runway, and I tried to look outside, but it was now pitch black. The pilot was given the go ahead to proceed, and the plane gathered speed down the runway. As the plane lifted off the surface of the runway, there was an almighty cheer and shouts from everyone with people clapping. We now knew we were finally on our way home, never to return to the desert again!

Blackadder insignia.

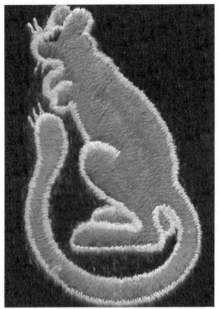

7th Armoured Brigade (Desert Rats) insignia, arm patch, Gulf War, 1991.

Epilogue

The Gulf war has been over now for 17 years. I wrote this book using the contents of the diary that I kept whilst on Op Granby. The reason for the length of time it has taken me to write this book was due to the amount of military commitments whilst I was in the army and the following transition into my civilian life, which was hard.

I thought the Gulf War was an invaluable experience for me as a soldier, but I felt it came too early in my army career because once I'd been to war and back, nothing else tops that. My personal feelings were that we did not finish the job, and we should have gone straight to Baghdad and got rid of Saddam Hussein for good. Another down point of the war for me was that I never got to fire my Gat in anger, which I would like to have experienced. I would do it all again if the need ever arose. In the end, the Gulf War turned out to be a big live firing exercise.

On our return to Germany, we were rewarded with four weeks leave for our efforts. Whilst on leave I married my fiancée, Paula, which wasn't planned but just happened because we didn't want to be apart from one another again; plus, Paula had gotten pregnant again with our first child.

I have a daughter, Natasha, who was born in Germany in December 1991 at the British Military Hospital Iserlohn. There was a big surge in military births in December 1991, and these children were referred to as 'Gulf War' babies. There was always a high birth rate in the army when any regiment has been away on a tour. I also have a son, Ryan, who was born in the army-married quarter in Feltham, Southwest London, in May 1994.

My army career lasted for 7 years in which I served in three different Royal Signals units, doing a soldier's job for real during the Gulf War; I opened my eyes to the attitude of ample amounts of the senior ranks within the Royal Signals. Because of their 'I'm alright Jack' attitude towards the junior ranks not only in war but also in normal barrack life, I felt the need to move on and that resulted in my transfer to the infantry. I then transferred to the 1st Battalion, The King's Regiment in 1994, which is my local infantry regiment.

Whilst I was serving in The King's Regiment I had to do a six-month tour of South Armagh, Northern Ireland in 1995. Further on, I terminated my services in 1996 while serving in Cyprus. Since my return to civilian life in 1997, I have mainly been employed as a plumber. I trained as a plumber as part of the army's resettlement programme to help ex-servicemen with the transition into civilian life. I have had medical problems that started about a year after the Gulf War finished. I cannot confirm that my medical problems are a direct result of my time in the Gulf, but I cannot deny it either, for numerous others have had medical problems too.

Paula and I are no longer together, due to her having an affair with a work colleague during 1999. Since our separation, Paula has made it difficult for me to have contact with my two children, and I have hardly had any contact with them since March of 2000. The family Court proceedings came to an end in 2007 with the result being that I have no contact with my children, which is very hurtful and not a day goes by without me thinking of them.

I did enjoy the majority of my time in the army and do feel it is a good career choice for any young person wishing to broaden their horizons, and I would like to take this opportunity to thank you for reading my account of an ordinary soldier's war.

Pete Molloy

Medals awarded from different governments for the Gulf War 1991
(left) British, (centre) Saudi Arabia, (right) Kuwait.

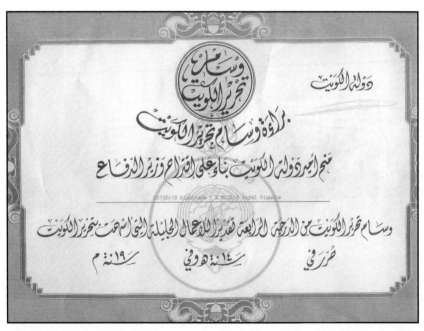

Certificate from the Kuwait government which accompanied the Kuwait medal.

Glossary

ADSR - Armoured Division Head Quarters and Signal Regiment

APC - Armoured Personnel Carrier

A.C.F. - Army Cadet Force

ADMIN - Administration

A.T.C. - Air Training Corps

BERGEN - Military Rucksack

BFPO - British Forces Post Office

CBA - Combat Body Armour

CEI - Communications Electronic Instructions

CIVVIE STREET - Life outside the armed forces

CO - Commanding Officer

COMMS - Communications

CND - Campaign for Nuclear Disarmament

CVRT - Command Vehicle Radio Tracked

DICKED - Told to do a shit job

DOBHI- Dirty Washing

DOSS BAG - Sleeping bag

DPM - Disruptive Pattern Material

EFI - Expeditionary Force Institutes

END EX - End of Exercise

EVHF - Elevated Very High Frequency

FEZ - Short for Festering. Someone who is Unclean

FMA - Force Maintenance Area

GAT - Nickname given to a personal weapon derived from the name of an air pistol

GPS - Global Positioning System

HF - High Frequency

IA - Immediate Action

ID CARD - Mod form 90 (Army)

JNCO- Junior Non-Commissioned Officer

MCO - Movements Control Officer

MFO - Military Freight Overseas

MLRS - Multiple Launch Rocket System

MP - Military Police

MRE - Meals Ready to Eat

MSR - Main Supply Route

NAAFI - Navy Army Air Force Institute

NAIAD - Nerve Agent Immobilised Enzyme Alarm and Detector

NAPS - Nerve Agent Pre-treatment Set

NCO - Non Commissioned Officer

NIG - New In Germany

OC - Officer Commanding

OP - Operation

ORDERS - Military Instructions

OSC - Operational Systems Control

PACKET - Group of Vehicles in a Convoy

PT - Physical Training

PTI - Physical Training Instructor

PX - American form of NAAFI

Q - Quartermaster

RAF - Royal Air Force

RAT PACK - 24-Hour rations

RECCE - Reconnaissance

ROASTIES - Roast potatoes

RSM - Regimental Sergeant Major

SALLY BASH - Salvation Army Shop

SAPPER - Nickname for a Royal Engineer

SCALEY - Short for the Royal Corps of Signals nickname of 'Scaley Back'

SCOUSE - A Person Who Comes From Liverpool

SEP - System Executive Plans

SGT. - Sergeant

SHF - Super High Frequency

SIG - Abbreviation for the Rank of Signalman

SLOP JOCKEY - Army Chef

SLR - Self Loading Rifle

SQUADDIE - Nickname for a soldier

SNCO - Senior Non Commissioned Officer

SSM - Squadron Sergeant Major

SSVC - Services Sound and Vision Corporation

STAFF - Staff Sergeant

STAG - Guard Duty

TA - Territorial Army

TN or TRUNK NODE - A mobile telephone exchange

TOMS - Nickname For A Private Soldier of the British Army (British Tommy)

UHF - Ultra High Frequency

UV - Ultra Violet sunrays

VHF - Very High Frequency

WRAC - Women's Royal Army Corps